MY CITY

Dear friend Simon: ⁵/₁₁
With good regards
& | " wishes

    Hoping to meet you
      Soon

    will phone from
    Spokane!

MY CITY ŁÓDŹ

POEMS BY M.J. GRANATSTEIN

Copyright © 1995

Front cover designed by Barbara Moore

The background of the front cover is the text of a morning prayer. The superimposed building is one of the major synagogues in Lodz which were razed when the Nazis arrived in the year of 1939.

The photograph of the author, on the back flap of the book was taken by George Brownell

CANADIAN CATALOGUING IN PUBLICATION DATA

Granatstein, M. J. (Morris Joseph), 1911-
　　My city Lódź

Poems.
ISBN 0-9680049-0-3

1. Lódź (Poland) – Poetry.　　2. Granatstein, M. J. (Morris Joseph), 1911- –
Poetry.　　3. Immigrants – Canada – Poetry.　　4. Poles – Canada –
Poetry.　　I. Title.

PS8563.R35M9 1995　　C811'.54　　C95-932410-0
PR9199.3.G73M9 1995

Tortoise Books
P.O. Box 69568
5845 Yonge Street
Willowdale, Ontario M2M 4K3

In Memoriam:

My mother and father, Dvoyre and Chayim-Itzchyk
and my three brothers, Beyrysh, Mechl and Layzer

For Barbara Moore, my good friend and
companion for her durable patience,
encouragement and goodness.

For my daughter and son-in-law
Ettie and Laizer Taichman for supportive
concern and understanding

For my grandchildren, Laura and Rebeca
for whom I wish, with all my
being, much happiness, joy and gratification
in all their endeavours

For my young friend, editor and critic,
Andrew Newman, with good wishes
for success and much pleasure in his
striving and work for his
doctorate in English literature.

For Stanley Bevington of the Coachhouse
for his help, guidance and unlimited patience
and understanding during the preparation
of my manuscript for this book.

Contents

M.J. Granatstein was born in Lodz, Poland in 1911. He immigrated to Canada with his mother, two sisters aged 11 and 4, and his 6 year old brother Layzer. Upon landing in the Canadian Port of Halifax in 1925 the family was detained by the Immigration and Layzer was deported back to Poland – accompanied by his mother, who left him with her sister in Lodz after a full year of leavetaking.

Layzer had been through a terrible ordeal of typhus just 3 months before the family set out on its journey to Canada. The illness left him with a stutter (more pronounced when startled or frightened) also a distinct limp... He was pale, thin and wobbled on his legs... "It was," G says, "as if he had nothing secure to stand on... He seemed to have stumbled into this world on an all-wrong keel... no leverage..."

The remaining children went on to Toronto, to join their father, who had already been there a full year – undergoing the tests and shocks of his new exile...

"So I wear my brother's scarred skin," G says, "live his short bereft life... over and over again... cradling words in the memory of my old Polish bye-bye..."

And this:

"Layzer is my repetitious nightmare, tangled into the haze of hallucinations about my City Lodz – now emptied of my brothers, my family... my people!!!"

And this:

"Poland, that Christian (Catholic) land of the celestial Family of Jesus-of-the-salve, Jesus-of-the-cross is also the land of DEATH CAMPS... In that Poland, during the initial years of the German Occupation, my entire family, consisting of some

eight hundred and more souls, was murdered by the Nazis and
the Poles, Nazis and Poles... there were no survivors."

"Moot questions of unbearable sadness: How do you say
Kaddish for eight hundred and more members of one's fami-
ly?.. How do you say Kaddish for one's murdered people?..."

The decades that have passed are not enough time for the
composition of such a Kaddish... We need new words and
there are no new words..."

When asked for an overall account of his checkered life on the
American Continent G shakes his grey head: "Difficult very...
Oy difficult!.."

And this:

"Messenger boy on a ten year old bicycle with patched
"inners"... distributing by the tens of thousands commercial
leaflets... working with my father: building leantos, porches,
sunrooms and installing the then absolute rage of high-high
fashion: "Picture windows," "Bay windows," "French doors,"
quarter-cut oak floors... and graining pine doors to look like
"Pine doors"... etcetera many many etceteras...

"Taught small children in Jewish parochial schools; lec-
tured in labor halls the disciplines of Marxism, Secularism,
Yiddish literature... wrote essays for left wing magazines and
newspapers... and poems for the drawers, satchels, pockets and
in countless rooms in Toronto, in rooming houses in
Manhattan, Brighton Beach, Philadelphia, Detroit and Havana
Cuba...

I attended, in my "spare" time available courses in
Toronto, in City College, NYU, the New School for Social
Research and thousands of hours in the hush of Public
libraries, without the slightest thought of attaining some kind
of qualifying Degree or title...

"After I was released (in 1945) from the Royal Canadian
Airforce I worked as an architect and later (beginning with the
fifties) as a Builder of housing and industrial and commercial
space."

"And dreamt a world without fear or hatred, a world of
tolerance and mutuality along the outlines of our great Biblical
prophets and Marx, Marx.."

Barbara Moore

ONE

The Baal Shem Tov of blessed memory
considered each letter of the hebrew
alphabet a complete living being.
One who fails, he said, to put the
proper concentration of mind and soul
into each letter of the prayer creates
a creature without limbs.

Propulsion

At times it was: *Hashiveynu Nazad,*[1]
which means regret
in dry weather, and wet... rippling

Hyndeh my Nana looked on
from under her brown coiffure
with its top baygl-bun.

I examined, from time to time,
ponderously, my fingers, toes,
puckered and unpuckered –
wisdom limpets, of my panoramic day

Guidelines, signposts, laws and
by laws, came later; at arms
length. During the twanging course
of limpid time. *Svet zayn git...* in outer world of salvation

And, *avadeh*[2], *mit Gott's helß*

Supervisory Dogma

> *Shacharyt, Myncheh, Maaryv*
> *Moydee Aanee,*[4]
> endlessly:
> In wonderment of symbolic
> centres, I tried
> to
> understand.

My sole preoccupation, over the years,
was building houses: large, medium and
small. With porticos, lean-tos, bay windows,
walls of glass, fantasy turrets where I
ate stolen apples, cheese, chocolate
dreamt bluish thoughts about sublime
princes with Torah Scrolls in
pockets, winter-birds on shoulders.

In sections of spaces, I met
knowledgeable angels with
systematic syntheses.

I conducted fearsome
dialogues in strange Alphabets
Full of knobby Isaiah heads striding
into lamentable eternity...

And, I was busy building
houses along unpaved roads, by-ways,
chained altitudes of
cutting heights.
 (Most especially in the
 Polish Karpathians.)

Glass walls, iron balconies, stone
untutored shapes, and
no two the same, with scissors that sheared
up and down with uncanny precision,
nothing the same.
Trying (succeeding) to destroy sameness
with drips and snags of multicolored
crayons, blobs.

Houses climbed up and down
spying on the King's
beautiful wife.

Spying on my Nana Hyndeh with
ample bosom and lullaby eyes.

Spying on my Uncle's one-horse
Droshkah, on beautiful blonde[5]
Veronika as she danced from
one *Kareteh* to another into the arms[6]
of uniformed officers of Polska's Republic.

Small and large houses of a rather unique style,
in huddling Jewish cities, towns,
villages, throughout the length and width
of Polska, Polanit, Poland, Poyln.
Our ethereal *o jczyzna nasza*, our fatherland, since
Kazimierz the great.

Wondrous vicissitudes: Pan Tadeusz
still with his boots on
striding from idiom to idiom
of emphasis, emphases.

Warshe, Lodz, Kielc, Lublin
Radom, Berdytshev, Konstantyin, Ivanck.

Zgierz, Vidzev, Chelm, Tarnopol and
Shoolym Aleychem's *Kasrilevke,*[7] where
goats nibbled on thatched roofs,
roosters with blood red combs crowed,
blind pigs snortled, rooting
for acorns round oak trees.

Now, from end to end, the houses,
Large and small are irrevocably
buried, dreaming pyramid
dreams... fizzing out along
perimetered mass-graves.

The above brings *Hashiveynu Nazad*
of the altogether, together again, again
by appointment and out of the shadowy
eaves of my mind: A diaper pin instead
of a lost button, a single rusted skate
fastened to a small boy's shoe.

A song clinging syllable
by syllable in baby wasp nests,
listening
through rigged silences
to *Haman* noisemakers.

Through ascension, descension,
by the essence of pilfered time,
over bumpy roads

Rusted skates
a rag football,
a wooden box of broken crayons,
a pair of winter earmuffs, my father's
hourglass, his worktable.

Passover Thaw

    January drifts
    February frosts,
    March waits for
    Passover thaw,

Vestige memories convulse.
Parkinson-like under lintels,
past door posts
locked doors,
wide-open rusting gates.

Into evil hush-baby darkness
round a cracked Greek Vase.
In penance.

    Penance means, not recreating,
    not transcending... It's not allowed.

My sister was afraid of the full moon,
or, of what's behind the full moon:
Murderers with sledge hammers,
frame saws, coal chisels.

Vermin and locusts, fantasy plateaus
on which children get lost;
never to return.

That is why, she said, the sun
sets on the other side...

The rusted gates are unhinged.
They tell ghost stories throughout
the night.

At sunrise my father donned his
prayer shawl, phylacteries,
and his neverface connected to
a spirit of song of ultimate strangeness.

The unhinged rusting gates began their
midnight's tic-toc *apocrypha.*

    I open and close my mind around the
    word, *Apocrypha,* but nothing
    happens. Only a repetitious
    litany of broken thoughts.

A rag doll my mother once made
for my sister Laytsheh got lost:
It reappeared at our doorstep
strangled with a rusted wire off a broken
fence.

On Winter Nights

On winter nights, round our parlour's
ceramic tiled oven, Reb Hersh our next-door
neighbour told complicated stories about
God's ante chambers.

The exile chambers of ethereal
anxiety, of infinite expectations.

Wrinkles, doodles, shrill voices,
down alleys, nooks, in which
burdened families lived under
rocks.

Angels of sleeping colours,
abruptly dishevelled
crossed the *Konstantiner* wings

Some kneeled at the gates of 7th
Heaven hammering their breasts with
stone wings:

Al Cheyt shechotonu lefonecho,
Al Cheyt,
Al Cheyt.[8]

Then gruesome descriptions of blood-curdling
sins. (some in parentheses.)

Some, full of sinking cadences,
rotating.
Calling our numbers, names,
for the new Biblia of martyrs with buffed backs

Also angelic stone stories
gathering behind Reb Hersh's wide
playtzes for angelic listeners with burning
ears.

Passover thaws came and went.
the times in-between were frequented
by Cyclops heads,
which claimed that the crises
will be over if we all meet in
the farmers square, called *Novy Rynek,*
where the *Chelmer* wait for us
to cleanse Jewish hearts and heads of
dandruffed sins.

One nice day of outstanding
levity and sunlight our teacher in
the Hebrew *Gymnazium* on *Wschdnia Ulitsa*
told us in hushed tones of voice,
(as if he were afraid of ghosts
in the squelched *Lodzer* streets)
about the Balfour Declaration.

The Baathon cloud structures
came and went. I came home
after school expecting the trunks
and *tshemendantshykes* packed and ready[9]
for our trip to *Yerusholayim...*

But my parents shook their heads
and looked at one another. My father
combed out his red beard with his
fingers and declared decisively:

We'll wait a while. There's no fire...
I looked in my father's eyes with
outstretched heart, arms:
     Fire!

I looked at my mother, accusingly.
It was she who sang over her
cast iron pots and pans
at the hot kitchen stove.

Oyfn veyg shtayt a boym
kroynen ungeboygn,
furt a yid kayn Eretz Isroel
myt farvaynte oygn.[10]
and patched trousers
and a cloak full of patches
and, a birch cane to slash the distance

Toothless grandfathers, grandmothers
ate out of careful spoons milk-soaked
crumbs of bread
hot steaming grytz.

Red cardinals flew back and forth
chirping lullabies for their
wide-beaked young.

Wandering minstrels played love songs
in overhanging branches

Covered wagons loaded with bunting,
Children, copper pots and pans
Rattled away into distances, waving
Goodbye.

In wagons: Gypsies
Rockbock, with ruined faces

I sit on my windowsill
With a tome of *Boove Kamo*[11]
In my lap trying to concentrate —
Footloose entertainers perform
In the courtyard below.

I sit on the windowsill
Waiting for the Messiah
with his new *Shulchan Oruch*[12]

My Zaide[13] sits at the kitchen table,
With pocket watch in hand,
Counting the minutes, moving
His blue shrunken lips:
"What's the matter with him?
It's late... He is late."

Below children skip rope, faces
flushed in glare of sunshine,
with total concentration.
Below Reb Doovydl's *kliatshe*[14]
Neighs,
a magician juggles
A dozen balls
Above a circle
Of upturned faces.

Below Veronika dances across the
Red square of the concrete slab
Waiting with bated breath

For a chariot in
Blueing wisp of *Boyadero*[15] smoke.

I see through my windowpane
Foaming emerald clouds,
Gathering round the pearly gates
Of Aarboth and Jericho.[16]

A white Konstantiner angel with a flaming
Sword slashes away
At puffs of unspeakables
Evil
Thoughts.

When I was two
I dressed in kingly raiment,
Damask and velvet from head to foot.
Threads of silver and gold circled my
Waist.

Phlegm-like caiques shuttled
Up and down my throat.

Motifs, stories, in separate
Cinematic frames: Are the dead really dead?
Do they lurk somewhere, between
Windowpanes, along the edge of the courtyard
Among the bluebottle flies.

I was Joseph manipulating
stars. Sorting relevances,
defining expectations.

With scrolls underarm, leftovers from
Beyond the Sinai peaks,

I was Aladdin with lantern
Lighting up the storied windows
Of the Konstantiner Courtyard. Up
The subdivided flats

My father danced a Gerer Rebbe dance
With prayerful upraised arms. It was not
Really a dance, it was more a somnambulistic
Shpatzeer into a *Yehuda*
Haleyvi world, onto his ship to the holy land.

My mother said: *Hefker the Velt.*
(it is a lawless world)
Candle light trembles on the ceiling.
Cracked veins show where pain
exerted too much stress. My mother
winds skeins of mercerized thread
on tinted wooden spools.

My father dozes over a page
of Caro's open book of
613 laws —

I already recited, frontally
by heart, my *Moydey Anee* lines
of inscrutability, and felt worse.

I try to re-catalogue my unspeakable
Misdeeds: A stolen winter apple
out of Mateleh Shlyoch's
crate. Trying to fake

a prayer I did not understand.
(Instead of *Kootn, Goodl,* instead of
laterally, frontally.)
A round little cardboard box of children's pistol
(Pulver) amunition placed upon streetcar tracks
in anticipation of a derailing explosion.

The beginning of doom
along a firing squad,
my mother's Russian romantic
songs as she pottered with
pots and spoons over her kitchen
stove.

Someone knocked gently on the front door.
Reb Hersh, our neighbour, with the
split white beard down to his chest,
brought a little canoe made of tree bark
for me.

For me?
For me.

He also came to discuss with me,
With me?
A page of Rashi.[17]
He was a Rashi specialist (bookey).

I read day and night, lines
    Between lines
    trying to figure the
    invocation of: "The
    Beginning of wisdom is, fear of
    God."

Does God require me to fear him?
What pleasure does He
derive from *my* fear? Does it help Him
with the FINALITY of
His judgment?

"The soul He injected into my
Being is in its total
state of purity" (etcetera)
"He is empowered to take it from me (etcetera)
when my time expires."
at His will... (etcetera)

What will He do in the name of eternity
with my soul? And what about my
Misdeeds? How will my soul manage before His throne
Will the angels laugh? weep?

And how will my mother, father, sister,
friends fare? Will they forget? Will they
grieve? Will they lie awake each alone
in their respective beds
weeping, wondering about my
New *Hekdysh* (situation) in God's 7th heaven?
Or will I (Godforbid) end up in *Gehenym*?[18]

Hosts and ghosts will rise out of their
graves, wiping their blind eyes with
skirts of their shrouds.
Ancestors will scuttle over whitewashed
fences, slide down beige mushroom roofs,
span the distances between the
Sinai, Babylon, Persia, Madrid, Barcelona,
the lowlands of Holland,
Ludka, Lodz with its

Passover-wine viscera,
    Waiting with pocket watch in hand
    for Messiah with his portfolio
    full of blue-haze plans.

I came upon my father's apprentice,
Yankeleh the Drong. He was on his
knees under an ancient acacia
tree declaring his everlasting love to
Hyndeh my Nana.

A strange spontaneous act beneath leafy
branches full of twittering birds,
coloured streaks, dots of sun, bright light
and trembling purple shadows.

The loving pair exists in mauve
oddness as they act out, movement by
movement their comical furious propulsions

    Hyndeh sits in the park on the green wooden
    bench with the fingers of her hands
    intertwined in lap, weeping.
    Why is she weeping?

Is it because of what Yankeleh
the Drong is telling her about his
eternal love? About certainty and uncer-
tainty, intertwined (like the intertwined
fingers of her hands in her lap)?

"Don't cry, no Hyndeleh, don't cry, no!"
said Yankeleh the Drong (on his knees) with
his chest at her knees,

"You are," he said, "breaking my heart, yes.
I had to tell you, yes, I couldn't stand it
any longer, yes. *Yiech hob gamaynt az yiech
Platz.*"[19]

> And if that was not enough
> Yankeleh the Drong takes her in his
> arms. Hyndeleh and Yankeleh
> suddenly seem
> totally intertwined: arms, legs,
> and Hyndeleh's ecstatic face
> raised into aura of green
> light.

Hyndeleh just weeps and weeps, gurgling
squawky little sounds in her throat as if she
had been transformed into a
fish out of water, gasping for air...

She then lifts her intertwined hands
over Yankeleh's brown tousled head of hair
(without separating the intertwined fingers)
and clasps him to her heaving breasts.

Draywagons creak over cobbled roads,
a horse neighs clopclopping in the cross-
silences of the Park. The horse
neighs again and again.

> I clench my hands and swallow
> salt, swallow by swallow,
> I step outside of myself and
> look into my eyes to view the
> effect of this wanton betrayal.

She was my Nana. A kind of biological extension
of my life, a balancing factor of my
tantrums... What will I do without the comfort
of her lap, arms, the lulling of her warm
breath as she whispers lullaby prophecies
of future days in mansions with gardens;
angels listening to *my* longings?
She was supposed to stay with *me* forever
and ever, and –
now the Drong!

On my way home I tried to figure,
step by step,
the essence of this criminal act:
chop off Yankeleh the Drong's
grotesque head. Or chop off his long legs, arms...

    With my father's wood-chopping axe,
    in an uppercut, while he is sitting
    on the *Kolye Gurtn* green bench waiting
    for Hyndeleh.

At home my father wants to know
where I spent
the evening? Did I say my prayers? *(Host gedavnt?)*
My mother wails,
"The child is starved!"

I said my *Moydey Anee* with a lump
in my throat. The lump grew and grew
in the tubular walls of the
interior of my neck...

I rose, stealthily, from my bed and entered
the toolshed to look at the axe.

I look and
my lump shrinks; I can
breathe again!

I then went to bed and dreamt a house
for my new morrow day.

1   *Hashyivenu* – Send me (Hebrew)
    Nazad – back (Polish)
2   *Avadeh* – Certainly (Yiddish)
3   *Mit Got's help* – With God's help (Yiddish)
4   *Moydey anyi* – I acknowledge [The Almighty] (Hebrew)
5   *Droshkah* – One-horse cab [for hire] (Polish)
6   *Kareteh* – Coach harnessed to horses (Polish)
7   *Kasrylefkeh* – Name of nonexistent town invented by Shulym Alaychem, the great Yiddish humourist. *Kasrylefkeh* represents all Jewish small towns in Eastern Europe (wiped out during the Second World War).
8   *Al cheyt shechotonu lefonecho...* – For the sins we have sinned against You (Hebrew)
9   *Tshemedantshyk* – Satchel (Yiddish)
10   *Oyfn veyg shtayt a boym kroynen ungeboygn, furt a yid kayn Eretz Isroeyl myt farvaynte oygn* – Along the road stands a tree with bent crown, a Jew travels to Israel with tears in his eyes
    Talmud talmudym – The sections of Rabbinic literature concerned with religious, ethical, civil and criminal law (Hebrew)
11   *Boove Kamo* – Section of Talmudic criminal law (Hebrew)
12   *Shulchan Oruch* – Table of 613 Laws (Hebrew)
13   *Zaide* – Grandfather (Yiddish)
14   *Kliatsheh* – an old skin-and-bone horse (Yiddish)
15   *Boyadero* – A Polish popular song
16   *Aarbot; Jericho* – Cities in Israel
17   *Rashi* – Medieval scholar, interpreter and commentator of Biblical texts
18 *Gehenna* – Hell
19   *Yiech hob gamaynt az yiech platz* – I thought I was going to burst!

TWO

Isaac:

*"Here are the fire and the wood
but where is the young beast for
the sacrifice?" (Genesis 22:7)*

Gyt Shabbys

Things schedule, sky
opens in downpour
days and nights tie together
by rhythm, refrain. My mother in her very embroidered
dress blesses the flames muttering without
sound her *Lehadlick neyr shel shabbys*[1]
Gyt Shabbys
Gyt Shabbys.[2]

With silver cups of shabbys wine in hands
Boyrey Pree ha'Gofen[3] in the draft of each
inherited *Neegn* (tune) without
destructing the cumulative concordant
effect my father with his Cantorial
yarmelkeh[4] with the thin smile with
knife in hand over the sacrificial
chaleh/shades of Abraham's *Akeydeh*[5]
in Samaria as little *Haman*[6] replicas
dance round the candle flames like –
Monarch butterflies.

In the courtyard all chintz curtained
windows are lit silver bright/no
smoke wafts from cold chimneys
magic candle flames flicker each time a door
opens/Beyrysh my brother does a little fancy
stepping as he changes seats with Mechl our brother/
learnt it from our father.

Gyt Shabbys
Gyt Shabbys.

Listen to the late hour
shuffling of ghosts through
wet dust.
Chazookeh, (power) in infinitude.

Shuffling feet under walls,
under street lantern gas-jet wheels
of light.

Lighting the way to
atrophied dry bones
nostalgic vagaries
of ghost tales
coming down from the rooftop/hills.

Dead dying witnesses
from widely distributed
areas flounder gears
steel teeth, in watchtower:
Watchmen with guns...

Bubbling up oxygen
razor-edge homesickness
from a world of
land of far-reaching fringes

At four worlds' ends.

Subsumed nightmares
gather moss, turn
into re-embroidered
dreams.

In dusty attics:
thrashed trophies, tarnished
medals, blind dolls without arms,
blind dolls without legs.

A pocket harmonica,
a guitar without strings,
toy guns, toy bayonets
a drum drums
1914, empty bullet casings
1914 gas masks.
1914 love letters
love letters.

There there there don't cry
your time will come,
out of magic that turns this way
and reverses,
your lullabies.

O empty your head of
Bundled fire-crackers –
of dread.

   Planets pass
   stars die
   in earth's sauna.

   Today, yesterday,
   shelved –
   rectitude specimens.

In jars, tubes, packed
in ice-salt
pressed leaves, flower petals,
named, sorted, numbered
in exercise books het-het.
So long ago, I forget forget.

Butterflies from
above the precipice
of cantilevered rock
flit.

I wrote somewhere
a reminder:

Do not weep.
Do not curse
the wind.

Mountains of Shoes

In Toronto – our new Canadian home
Mendl the house painter
stands with pail of paint in one hand and a ladle
in the other.

One minute,
two minutes,
three.

Mendl like a monument caught in
camera's lens forever.

"Mendl, Mendl!
What's the matter?
Every drop has drained out of
your face.
Should I shake you?"

Mendl shakes himself.
"Ooooh Moishe... If my youngest
son were alive today... he would be
twenty-seven years old... Today
is my Shoolym's birthday..."

Camera night lens
Focused on a neat
mountain of cracked
dried-out shoes

    Children shoes
    Women shoes
    Men shoes
    Boobeh-Zaideh shoes.[7]

The rats got the socks,
the rats swallowed the
nails, the soles.
Two rats are dead in
one big shoe.

The rats are at the bottom
of the mountain, rustling
squeaking.
Bing, ding goes the
end of shoe lace.

Canes, canes
tarnished rings,
scattered watches without
innards,
in between in-and-out
under ghastly walls.

Miscalculations Calculations

Grey sparrows squat on a taut
laundry line strung across
wing-to-wing, on pulley-wheels.

Gossip about an epidemic of
German measles

    An epidemic of flu
    polio, arthritis, brain fever.

An owl on a lone acacia
hoots about
tangled daydreams.

In slippery dank tunnels
shredded words words fill the
atmosphere with *haggadahs*

German-Polish Parallelograms

O for a green and short life
within sight of Polish
green valley
parallelograms, peeled.

Not too far from O my city Lodz
engineers, surveyors pound into the
ground corner stakes, squared iron stakes and cribs
for barracks, bunkers, administration
quarters, rows of shower halls prison walls
cleanliness *macht das leben züss.*

Good husky shturm-boys. When they issued
commands their harsh shrill guttural voices
made the Polish women swoon...

O ojczyzna moja[8].
Handcuffed unto vile dreams
jestesz you are like health
as long as we live,
survive – you will live... live!

Sto lat, a hundred years
with hammered steel breastplates,

A thousand years of meddling
with
herbs and moss
over missile-resistant gods

Connecting dark forests
down the plateaus of the
Polish Karpathians.

Iron knuckles tap the transparencies
inside my skull:
Maciek the strurz on his bench
Zygmund the courier-pigeon-man,
high up on the roofs.

The Polish barber with the
clippers in his hand
clipped clean
my seven year old head.

And O my father with
his iron bar smashing mirrors
As Abraham smashed gods...
mirrors on the walls
up front and behind
as he turns his legs like
an upside-down V wide apart.

Mirage maidens with
accordian skirts
legs that turn like
trundles inside the
vineyard fence of the promised land

Come, come down the mountain
from the other side
See how we on this
side live

Holes instead of eyes,
Pits instead of ears,
blind nameless skulls
Where did you live.
Where do you live.

and I in passing seem
insignificant

Rainbow Coloured Coat

The hammering in my head
inside the concave walls
of Joseph's

Twelve-star dream

In the snakepit he corners
single-handedly
a family of mourning
boa constrictors

My brothers
are going too far down the road of
franticness... boa constrictors!!!

Are afraid of the stranger come
from Eden with smoldering
hypnosis-eyes;
are momentarily
paralyzed.

Joseph's luck
concentrating on the
one-in-a-million chance
by

Sewing together words, legends,
        Crutch metaphors
        Malediction
        Bafflement.
Seven over seven
by seven, in spiral dance

46

As his (not so?) proud little
brothers arrive at the
gates on
          Donkeys
          Elephants
          Camels
Bearing gifts...

At night Joseph suffers
an attack of mammoth gout.

He rises, with difficulty out of his four-post
ebony bed,
opens the trunk
and there it is, the
          many-coloured coat

Give me this night
to end the seven-year-
itch...

Blue and white strips of
Egyptian linen float like
boas in Joseph's head.

(The boas – themselves escaped
from a fiery furnace – knew
enough to stay in their corner
under concave snakepit
walls.)

O if father Ya'akov were
here now... Ya'akov...

We could tell one another
the wildest stories and sing,

O Hashiveynu nazad
in a hot tub of bi-carbonated
Giza wine...
Shades of the baker, the
wine keeper
with ordinance dreams in
Pharaoh's kitchens

And ponder under the stars
about unfathomed sphinx
mysteries

And talk under the stars
about sphinxed mysteries

O gedichte[10]
O lieder
O Geshichteh

And along a new theme:

How could my
brothers recognize me
when I hadn't shaved
in twelve years?

Also:
What happened to Benyumyn?

The hammers, the hammering,
    Kling-klang
    kling-klang

As if an impatient visitor
with jade-triton horns
wanted in?
or out?

Seven swans
seven silos along
the Nile.

Hieroglyphics of lightness
kings with gold beads
seven Giza sphinxes
seven Giza tablets.

Twelve stars raised in heads,
upon the diagonal tier
of brooding
sequestered
kings.

The stars
dispersed.

The many-coloured coat
turned into a laudatory
drudge with

    a nose like a *Kashtaniec*[12]
    ears like Eagle wings,

Fingertips stretched to touch
the rising sun.

The drudge
stood in the frame of

the window with open mouth
to ponder the outrage
of a Nile turned from green-blue
into
purple-red blood – already?
under a climbing sun.

The sun was already high
above
in the
middle.

Joseph issued his noon-command
in a ringing *haresh:*
"Let them wait at the gate...
There is no rush..."
"How long?"
"I will let you know..."

He then wrote painfully
(in picturesque arthritic
script) his last and final
testament.

sealed in blue wax

"When you leave this Egypt
land and its *Mitzrym*
(soon or not so soon)
O little *Chooshyveh* brothers[13]
O Ya'akov's sons,
O brothers

Take my moldering *Oodoomic*
bones back
to Canaan

Twelve upon twelve
greening dreams are over there
waiting
for me.

Signed: *Joseph, your brother.*

The Courthouse Ladder

Pry, pry apart the
welded door of my
memory.

And out with it in the light
of the irreducible square
at the foot of the
courthouse ladder...

There a glum judge sits on a
Polish footstool
with a putty face,
Shoe-button eyes,
little arched *grablie*[14] hands
on his knees

And God (god again) on
throne above
surveys the rubble,
the invisible walls,
the vanished windows,
the idiot eyes

Out and out
of the corners
in late judgement.

Morning light
filters through
curtained windows.

Orphaned children wipe
their eyes and cry
Orphaned children
don't cry.

An adult couple in a flat
above our flat
fantasize staring into one
another's eyes.
Blue and green crosses
comb each other's thoughts

Caruso Island, an eagle nest
on an inaccessible mountain
top.

Himalayas, Alps,
in the light of
what they rebelled against unilaterally

As the fairy tales grind down
didactic fantasies, a pine stump,
a pine memory
generations of birds
droll drool zingersing

Dreams of chastened lives
along tramway route
the Greek Josl Sitacles across the courtyard
in a one bedroom flat. From along the
Ionic gulf. Considered himself a
Taulatnian descendant
of an Illyrian race

his wife was a Jewess, a member of
a Bundist Party Cell.

Sitacles claimed to have been
blessed by a dynastic Rebbe of Vroclav.
Therefore invulnerable.
In the meantime
he plied his trade as bookbinder
in a basement room on Wschodnia.

At night students gathered in his
workshop to listen to
poetry readings: Yeats,
Joyce, Tuvym,
Konopnicka, Catafi, Alaixandre.

As Veronika danced around the
bookbinder's bench, Jo Sitacles
read Cocteau

My uncle and
Meeme Chaye
attended on Wednesday nights.

Laibysh

In the City Kolye Gurtn [garden]
prevalence of exhausted green
Trees grass weeds reeds benches
green

A middle aged man
in kneehigh leather boots
pumps way away
on a bicycle
from anywhere to
everywhere

In the park
Laybysh Yoine's only son
sits on a green bench
Schoolcap with shining black visor
too tight on oversized
outsized brown head

Head full of awkward prophecies
like colliding trains
gone berserk
in wind fire and sand

He holds a Zohar
in one hand
and Das Kapital
in the other

    He places Das Kapital
    across his lap
    and the Zohar on top

He then slashes both his wrists
with pocket penknife
      pocket penknife
      pocket penknife

On the green bench
in green exhaust

      Oh
      You gave us this day
      this one hour this moment
      before the sun wentdown
            the sun wentdown
            the sun wentdown

While, my friend, Laybysh bled dead
in the green dark
of the Kolye
Garden

she'hecheyonu ve'kimonu...
(that we have lived
to see this day.)

High up on the roof
alongside a four-flue chimney stack
a solitary stork
stands on one
orange-coloured
leg

On the top balcony stands
a young maiden in a red apron, red cheeks
with splayed bare feet
in concrete dust

It is not
difficult
all I have to do is close my eyes
and the green years
roll by
roll back by

Seasons in joy
    in sadness
    almost
    almost
    almost

Courtyard plaints
    songs
    laughter
shuffle through
from all four corners
from window to wall to rubble

The maiden on the balcony
Beats a green rug
with a rug beater
clasped in both hands.

    On a grey square of
    cobble dust Masha the cat
    plays with another chanced mouse

Grey on grey, yellow on yellow

The gray mouse tumbles
between cat-paws
like a ball of
mouse dust.

In between it pretends to
run away but it knows:
no prayers, no mercy, no
reprieve
only little tin-tin tiny squeaks.

Words are inadequate along gurgling
gutters, street-corner legless beggars
with hands between stumps vagaries in
eyes across high facade mirrors
windowpanes of long since banished images

Hersh the Konstantiner is looking for
listeners the first half, the second, the
third in invisible monochrome/the Polish
barber holds me down with one elbow/
into my midriff/memories burn
down as the mirrors tinkle irregular shards
at my feet

Three Poles smirk jabbing each other in
ribs/my father points, "Is that him?" I nod.
My throat is blocked, I see Chai in a long
line, single file as she approaches a female guard

In an agonized moment I chopped off the barber's head
before I woke.

Chai did not say goodbye/the clippers began
clipping at the back of my neck and all the
way round my skull stopped at my forehead
the barber grinned showing a mouthful
of crooked teeth
"Tell them," he said,
"tell them a red and white diagonally painted
barber-pole told me I will
see you in your Hebrew paradise."

I chopped his
head off
again.

with dandelions in her brown hair Chai
said goodbye through tears
when the bridge was
raised she was nowhere.

Colliding waves of nausea rose from the
pit several tunes that stay with me
the way he walks with his head to
the left full of categorical anomalies
Chirugiczne stories by a great Australian
surgeon who will float kites as Beyrysh climbs the ladder
into a cloud

The Polish barber held me down with one
elbow in my midriff I squirmed
afraid he would clip off my ears

My father glowered at my clipped skull. He said,
"Take me to your barber!"

From the green iridescence of my Zaide's Polish
wood father brought an iron bar used to
fasten the window shutters into iron slots
Chai walked with her head up in the rays of
the sun
she approached the polish guard
her face already yellow
at the prospect of showerjets

The barber-pole at the entrance/the word
(Davar) pulled down the ladder in the courtyard
from under Beyrysh's feet
the sections of the bridge raised and
collided with sunbeams
threatening with grim shadow a fence with
climbing roses
My brother is already
beyond the top rung up to his waist
in a melancholic cloud.
He lights firecrackers instead of
fiery expletives of distress/my mother sits in her
deeprush chair at the side of the stove singing
Kinderyurn majneh shaineh blumen
she is knitting a blue sweater
for me

The bubble of quicksilver at the
centre of the level dissolved
sucked into the levelled wood.

The plumb dropped.

60

The ladder lost its plumb
creaked from foot to head and
dropped, down the wall
into the milkman's window...
into the milkman's window

A pack of wolves ran through Konstantyin
towards the Novy Rynek looking for little
Jews inside the bubbles of quicksilver.
Red rimmed eyes flittered
in the sockets as they bayoneted
stacks of hay and straw.

Yankl the drayman stood in the doorway
scratching his head with one hand
and another:
"What? What, What!"
Hent rauf.[15]

Later Yankl's little boy
wanted to know
the whereabouts of his father
and where are our horses?

His mother took him to
a field full of square and
oblong stones.
"There, underneath your father sleeps."
Your father sleeps
Your father sleeps

My father said, "Suddenly, just like
that..."

He wanted to know what I was doing
in the middle of the week in his
workshop?

"Today is Wednesday, no?"
"Yes."
"Nooo?"

He then two-step-side-stepped
tweaking his nose between green stained
fingers resuming the humming
of a nasal tune fresh from Ger[16]

I had to talk loud so he could hear me
over the whirring creaking
and singing of the looms.

The windows were open we could hear
iron-clad wheels rattling over cobbles,
chanting voices of eager merchants

I told him I came to fetch/
for my Zaideh/some paper
nibs, ink and a Sayfer... (book)

I told him I came to see you 'my father'
for three or four or
five Zlotys, ha ha ha?

My father pinched my cheeks
and
laughed, ha ha ha.

My father's feet bled profusely

He would rest on the
top tread of the steps of the
dark Wylker synagogue

He bit his bruised multicoloured
knuckles, rejecting
the structures of
disembodied walls
up front and side

I reminded him that it
was late Friday night
and how did you get here
all those thousands of miles
on a Friday night?

He said he came to pray in his
old Wilker synagogue *(shul)*

My Chai skips rope and laughs:
she laughs,
I laugh,
my mother laughs.

My mother laughs but she is blind.
She asks, "Has anything
changed? Is everything the same?"

Chai chants:

Piervsva godzina i bonk szpi
It is one o'clock and the Bonk sleeps.
Druga godzina i bonk szpi
Trzecia godzina i Bonk szpi

It is one o'clock
It is three o'clock...

As her feet weave in and out
the rope...

Robins chirp in the maple
at the wall

My mother:
Come and climb,
Moisheh it's your last
chance... The sun won't
stand still.

She says:
I have no regards...
They're all in little
baskets trying to sort out
their memories:

Where have they been? Where, where?
What have they seen? seen, seen...
They draw red roses
in the air, distribute them
among
lady bugs,
snap swallows
and robins

They all say: no, not, no not tot

Did you see your father?
I can't see him.
I am blind you know...

When I left he was still sleeping
in the foliage,
under an oak
under the
wall.

The Wilker Shul

In my dream everything lives
on edge and my father's feet bleed
as he rises two steps at-a-time to the

top of the invisible steps of the
Wilker Shul
he then stops to
rest one step down from the invisible
landing his knobby knees
are at the sides of his cheeks
as he removes the shoes

And the socks with eyes fixed
on a former window of a

Former wall following the train of a tune
beedy-dim-bombym sense of
melody of being in this place of

Unease/as he bites the knuckle
of his hand rejecting the vision
of rubble and hills

I remind him that it is Friday
and late/all the stars that are
                out are out two million times
                two million stars celebrating the sabbath

"And by the way tateh how did you
manage to get here from the otherside
of the ocean?"

He came here, he says to pray just once more

Before he dies???

My mother arrives with a basket
on the hook of her arm
she wears the same old coloured kerchief
on her greying head,
she remembers scents

Father and mother are of course
totally invisible to
everyone but me

Except Chai who skips rope on an
overturned obelisk a little to the
left of the highest rubble mound

She laughs
Mother laughs in her singing voice
Chai sings sings:
eighty eighty-one eighty-two
and:

Will you help us find our way
back to the dead?

Still skipping:
eighty-seven eighty-nine ninety ninety-one

Mother says:
"I am blind you know."
Mother wants to know if I am still
wasting "Are you?"

All those dumb dumbest years
        dumb dumbest sorrows
my thoughts turn into tatters
        turning

        Time in wasteland
                in quick march
                easier at ease
                on bleeding feet

Just once around the square of four blocks
                and the blood
inside tightfitting shoes thickens

I fit my prayers into shoeboxes
together with wrongsize shoes
on the old windowsill my windowsill

Chai chants:
Piervsza godzina i Bonk szpi[17]
It is one o'clock and the Bonk sleeps
druga godzina i Bonk szpi
trzecia czvarta
i Bonk szpi

Legs weave in and out
in the shimmer of her hoop

Mother sings an otherworldly song
about pontoons lakes drownings
death by water by hunger by longing
by lack of air by homesickness...

Father says he forgot his Tfylyn
"But never mind God will understand
I can pray naked and shoeless just the way
I am *Ashrey yoyshvey Bayseychoh oyd
yehalelyicho seylo...*

Happy are Those who Dwell in Thy House

Words ring as of old
but the meaning changes changed
within the marrow of the words
standing at attention
still on bleeding feet
      Ashrey yoyshvey
      Those who dwell

Czvarta godzina i Bonk szpi
on the highest rung in a cloud
in your house
in your world

In the middle of
unstoppable words
rain
hail
out of emptiness

No easier
through dead walls of no access

My *Mameh-Looshn*[18]
(Mother tongue)
brought to reckoning
My covenant
the light behind her eyes
out the one window

Rolled tight on my father's
wooden miracle spools

Host gedavnt? (Did you pray?)
Davenen gedavnt
and the prayers across the city into Balut Ghetto

Prayers carved into four solitary walls
of memory

The sound of it the sound
in head

As voices and distances increase
                              increase

All I need do is close my eyes
listen to the grass grow
leaves shush in breeze

And the years rollback
and roll back
as blood circulates

Mother sits on the ottoman
at the open window
the chintz curtains billow
into the sounds of the courtyard

Solitude and sadness entwined
like a two-ply rope
breathless
almost

My mother sings,
the courtyard below
weeps:

Shchyneh Shchyneh[18A]
how far are you?
exile exile
how large are you?

In the Rynek
a Maypole hung with
folksongs
laughter laughter
and laughter woven into
curses

Curses
woven into laughter

Together with wishes praises
        Sto lat sto lot
        a hundred years of merry life
        and merry life

"Eirisione brings figs figs and fat loaves/
honey in a jar and a cup of strong wine
to drink herself to sleep."

In Bays Midresh my Zaide sits at a wooden
table pondering
secrets in folds
of myths

He moves words up and down
from here to there
and here

But the myths hold fast

Someone knocked on the door
early in the morning
Someone knocked in the
middle of the night

But no one heard no one
and no one, not even when it stopped

My father twosteps on his way to the Wilker
synagogue face in myth
drawn in indelible ink

Wrapped in heavy lidded sorrow
wrapped in cottons silks gaberdine linen
cheviot vygunie

Combed cotton washed and blessed again again

      The shchyneh the shchyneh
      would not be so far
      if the exile
      the exile
      were not so large
      and not so large

When Lilyth enters my room
I close my eyes
and count to thirty

And say the Shema
and another Shema
and a third Shema

Good night good night
and goodnight

73

1 *L'hadlyk ... Shabys* – Mother's blessing over Sabbath candles (Hebrew)
2 *Gyt Shabys* – Good Sabbath (Yiddish)
3 *Boyrey ... Goofen* – Blessing over wine (Hebrew)
4 *Yarmelkeh* – Skull cap (Yiddish)
5 *Akeyda* – Abraham's sacrificial altar (Hebrew)
6 *Haman* – Evil Purym character
7 *Boobeh Zaydeh* – Grandmother/grandfather (Yiddish)
8 *Ojczyzna moja* – My fatherland (Polish)
10 *Gedichte* – Composition (German)
   Lieder – Songs, poems (German)
   Geshicte – History (German)
12 *Kashtan* – Chestnut (Polish)
13 *Chushyv* – Honoured (Hebrew)
14 *Grablye* – Rake
15 *Hent Rauf* – Hands up (German)
16 *Ger* – a town in Poland, of Rabbinical fame
17 *Bonk* – one who oversleeps
18 *Mamelooshn* – Mother tongue (Yiddish-Hebrew)
18A *Shchyneh* – God's presence (Hebrew)

THREE

"A man a writer, whose bones
fitted themselves together and
came to life after extinction
now sits in a corner little by
little putting things down on paper."
                    – Nathan Alterman

My Brother Mechl Left me his Silk Top Hat and Two White Rabbits

Your silence Beyrysh blots
the dumb circle on my dumb page
Passing from rock to rock
of calcified selves

Not even an accidental
Deaf and mute postcard
from you or Mechl, from the USSR

Varständlich?

As you were once fond of saying:

> *Unvarständlich*
> *Unvarständlich*[1]

While I here turn and turn
And every night
through and between
Iron bars in the windows
I see a burdened slope
under the same
Stars

Banked-in hieroglyphs
of luminous black ice and snow

And the city outside
thuds over cupped dams
in wonder of disorder
vindicated in ferment.

Remember our father:

"...any leaven that may still
be in the house which I have
seen or have not seen shall
be as if it does not exist"

sustained

Or exists and bleeds
in my dream-country Poland Lodz

In trembling flickering
candle-light

In reverence of God's
dust of departure

Rasp of breath in chest
An exercise book in yellow
classroom light
A day book in leather
bound covers
asleep somewhere
in a bed
of marigolds

Leaven bread crumbs
strategically distributed
in corners niches
the beginning
and end
of memorial event
on the final day before Passover

My name carved
with mother-of-pearl penknife
onto my classroom desktop

A draydl coloured *strulkes*[2]
A sheaf of poems

Windows and flowering
sunset flame a
fairy tale of ice

In windows pale faces of
yearning fathers over a Zohar line
Line after line of word-fascination
in an ocean of
Gematria[3]

Mateleh Shlioch's baskets of
jerzelkes[4] pears winter apples
september tomatoes

Plots shrugged off
shining armour a famous white horse
a jade bridge
over a green ravine

All of it turns
through year-end turnstiles
singing *Shtille Lieder*[5]
Shtille Lieder

Now tucked away in a
hip pocket of eternity's
misplaced
Trousers

I am Planning a Hannukah Party

I am planning a Hannukah party for Layzer and the
Latvian orphaned children in detention
by way of *Esther ha'Malkhah*[6]
Ahausveyraus's beloved on the edge
of a ridge of *sypurym massioths
maisalech*[7]

Lou Krawczyk, seven years old, is building a chariot out of
toothpicks and burnt matches – he needs
wings and a coat of invisible paint
also two hacksaws, one for me, one for him
to escape along the centre of the corridor's
fly-specked ceilinged seasons

Lou, one of the orphans says, "Moy Sheh please show you
teeth." which means, smile

Two white rabbits
half alive
half dead
sit on my head

They stare at me
out of a dark mirror
of memory with
violet rabbit-eyes

Like two wool skein
rabbit sculptures

Dream of Execution

"*Tateshyi tateshyi* (Daddy)
I will now ask you the four
famous questions."

"Why is this night
different from all other nights?"
Why?

One rabbit in the dark mirror
wears my blue *kippah*[8] the other
wears my school cap with the shining
                    visor

Delighting in themselves
In the dark darkly...

I dreamt the other day
that my tongue had cleaved
to the roof of my mouth
in punishment.

In the distance muffling
sounds of sleighs
barking dogs chugging trains
into the dark of – punishment

My school cap is too small
for my head it cannot cover
the white rabbits Mechl left me
I had to use his silk top hat

81

Where is Mechl?

I dreamt a *kretshme*[9]
I always dream *kretshmes*
with cowboys who speak
Buffalo Bill language

      Outside horses neighed
      Voices of water carriers
      Yuhooooed
      whips exploded like gunshots
               gunshots

On the wall behind the bar
a clock turned
its hands

Without stopping

two *czynovnikes*[10]
in uniforms brought in you my brother
in chains
You threw back your shoulders and
          Shouted:
"No blindfolds!"

They placed a gag in your mouth
And tied a red kerchief
round your eyes

You pointed your chin at me
As if it were my fault

Al cheyt she 'Chatonu le 'foneycho[11]

What fault, sin?
What did I do?

When they removed the gag
in your mouth you said
          through blue squashed lips:

"It is not his fault
he did what I told him
to do."

"What?"

"Remove my blindfold...
I have to memorize your faces..."

The tall brown man
with the tall red hat
said:

"What do you do?"
"I play Buffalo Bill on the stage
of the Scala theatre in Lodz..."

"What did you do?"
"I studied the Bible on account of a
promised *Chumysh*[12] party..."

"What did you do?"
"I thanked the *Reboyne shel Oylom*[13]
at every step..."
"God's steps?"
"No no no my steps like

Baruch ha'Shem,
Baruch ha'Shem."[14]
"Step by step?"
"Step by step."

"What did you do?"
"I stole *jerzelkes* out of
Matl Shlioch's *jerzelke*-basket."

Will someone prop me up? My feet
are numb the mushroom wall over my
head is collapsing into the mushrooms
beneath the giant pines in my
Zaide's Polish wood.

This stanza is not from memory
it is from actual notes I had once taken/
when I woke in the morning it was time
To say *Shacharyt* and then
school I told you what I dreamt and you
told me to write it down I wrote it down
and here it is word for word: the carrier
pigeons rose from the roof and I went to school
to recite Nakhman Bialik also the first ten
paragraphs of *Lech-Lecho* get going.[15]

Wind in the flames
of the thorn bush

Cold fire hot fire
Still the bush sleeps through it
God in the flames of
the thornbush
"This letter is:
chugging hieroglyphs

chugging steel
wheels
over
Steel tracks

Praying for miracles

God looks at me:
'I did it once ha ha ha'
'never again ha ha ha'
Still a camel caravan
is dying of thirst
I too am dying   if I should die
                        if I could die."

An old man on a trapeze
watches with binoculars the
lengths of the shining tracks

Trains come and go
slicing the darkness
into slices of dreams

The old man on the trapeze
is counting the fingers of
his hands

ains
tzvay
dray
fyier[16]

Two of his fingers
are missing in his
right hand
He has eight fingers

Trains come and go
Chugging loneliness homesickness
between wheels
on tracks.

Each wheel equal and alone

People come and leave
triangles circles and
squares of memories

I shall recognize their faces
Even though they are
shadows

I recognize
a dark man with broad shoulders
waiting for a train
with his right cheek
on the track repeating
in his head: goodbye
                goodbye

He says:
"They will know why I came
they will part the shadows and
lament over   spilled grain
                       spilled blood
                       the pillars
                       the torches
                       the ugliness

"They will want all everything
I can still spare
They will say:

'*jak było tak było*'[17]
What was was
They will say 'button up your shirt'
They will say: '*panie.*'"

What else?

Only memories of torches in colours of twilight

The red little Jews from the
other side of the Sembatian river
got my foreskin

There is a strong scent of
Lilac
Lilac trees
and the scent of clover

From a nearby gorge

bellflowers in the onrush
of wind

There are no lilac trees,
There is no clover,
There are no bellflowers

I sit on a stump
on the other side of the field
of wheat smoking my first
Polish cigarette

Smoke like a mixture of
horse radish
and chroset

burns the lining of my
throat

I smoke and gag
inhale exhale as you Beyrysh
taught Mechl once

Ribbons of blue smoke
like kite tails
float away over my shoulders
into the elegance of a
sunsetting event

Ribbons of blue smoke
over one shoulder
then another
as I move the cigarette
from one corner of mouth
to the other

The sound of a distant buzzsaw:
astounding proclamation
of foregone conclusion gone...
The sound of a felled
Giant pine tree is a thud
of devastating dread foregone

It is as if the buzzsaw
in my Zaide's wood was sawing
at my skinned being

Then the dreadful thud
splits my head
in two in three

A train whistle stops
my breath

The man on the track
the track under the man's head
in distant procession

I throw away my cigarette
and wait for the Messiah on-off-track

My Zaide

It gets down to what
my Zaide told me
in his summer hut:

About possibilities
choices between
illumination and
darkness

      And the godliness of knowing and
      understanding:

Legends
Legends have only
one mask

Legends have many masks
ill masks
sane masks
evil masks
happy masks

Deferential possibilities
forward backward down up

An open river in my head
along clay walls carries a full red
moon

Round a sudden idiom turns into the
arms of a willow of green velvet

In dreamtime in a painting
on a windowed wall that is not
a wall but an opening
into a wild prophetic river

my dark pockets are not empty
they are filled to the brim with
pocket-gods who make room
for my hands

"It is told in the passover
Hagadah," my Zaide with his passover
hand on his gray beard intones

"...that even if we were all wise all wise
all men of understanding and even

if we were old and
well   learned
                learned

it would still be our duty
to tell our future generations of
the Passover debacle..."

what we saw

before the heart of the attic
was pulled down in thunder of accolade
on top of the outerspace in our courtyard
Before the ladder
with its crawlspace
went down

And even though
we are dead tired and
at Your mercy

Gaping wide-eyed into the
unknown wide eye
from here and
over there/
there are still legitimate descendants of
Samuel's chosen kings

Rolling into an abyss arm in arm
legs entwined listening to the
thunder of your
storm as when we were
totally alive
in the godliness of time.

It is as my zaide said, "*Harey
Zeh mashuboch.*"[18]
"The more life is to be praised"

With swamped bladder.

Whatever I turn turns into lace-trimmed
bobbin-weave

Shades and sounds of my father's gallery of
textile bolts

hands and arms
dip in dye
shuttles pound yarn
into place

Threads over poles
in musical blend
borrow stress from
instruments
thread inside soul
rising lifting in
folds of silence aligned shadows

memory takes me to where
my cribbed life
exists only in
unfolding regrets
continue in dark fields
driven by long beams of swift
cutting tracks

The pocket gods are gone
escaped through a hole
in the bottom of the pocket –
holes in
the linings...

Puts me in mind
of Mechl
you'd think you have
him cornered at the end of a dead street
but when you get there
he is somewhere else
always somewhere
else in blue air

Prophecies of things to come – come
Nathan in King David's
throne chamber
saying, "You are a man"

93

not a god...

Nathan crossing over to receive
the blessings of a tattooed
messiah

Poles with uneasy conscience complain
of sleepless nights

hilarious little Polish provocateurs
in Jewish backyards courtyards
in Jewish attics
in basements
dig dig

scheme plot rub-rub
hands together

A Jewish family of eight for a sewing machine

a synagogue full of atoning Jews for
a sack of flour (mixed with straw)

A grand piano for my Meemeh Chaye
and her daughters:

 Laye Sonia Geetl Chaveh

And Chaye's jewelry:

 buried under a cobble marked X
 on a map

Another Letter:

You Beyrysh pulled
my first wooden sleigh
into a snowbank

You showed me King David's
face in a snow-*zaveruche*[19]

Mechl hammered together
my second sleigh called:
Boyberyk-on-steel-runners

Do you Beyrysh know
if Mechl got himself
a new top hat?

Let me sleep beneath your
yoke's bow in my bruise

Across a maze of the
unstoppable scream
in my blood

Show me your covenant postings
are they the same as mine?
in the light of the blade
of Abraham's knife?

In the unattainable eternity
symbolisms:

I step out of myself
step over myself

blinded by the midday sun
Weeping in particles
of ashes dust
gathering god's pain

God's pain seeps through
Holes in crates

At the gates of my initial days
in Lodz
Balut
From Balut to Osviencieh
in cattle boxcars as

Poles guard sealed sliding doors

Authorized under
hakenkreux authority[20]

Polish guards smirk up
at Jews climbing into
        boxcars

with upraised chins
and one stiff hand
sawing across throat
the other pointing up
at terror-faces:
        es müss zein[21]
        koniecznie!

O Polska moja ty jestesz jak zdrovie[22]
Na zdrovie
Na zdrovie
Now that the ice is broken

Mendl the Housepainter – Again

Mendl named his newborn
Canadian children after
his firstborn children
in Kielc Poland

After their eyes in silent repose
visioned through barbed fence
thrashing before brass (musical)
instruments

At bedtime Mendl walks from bed to bed
in his new house in Toronto Canada

Hoisting his pants: nerves
Rubbing his eyes with
the knuckles of his fists: nerves
pulling one hand down his chin
on the nonexistent beard: nerves

lyou lyu lyou lyu   sleep   sleep
Ay lyu lyu lyu ay! oy!

Against
Nightmares

He says:
"Now Moishe time enough...
Will you join me and my
family this Saturday night
at Benny's Hideaway for
blessings and a good dinner and
a bottle of good wine

In the meantime he lets it
sleep in the bit of new happiness
under the double *peryne*
"...me and my good wife Frymeh..."

From bed to bed:

Good night Getzeleh...
Good night Shloymeleh...
Good night Hayiml...
Good night...   My *shayne Shayndeleh*[23]

With his knuckles of one hand then the other
between his teeth

He then climbs into his bed under
sheathed tent
with Frymeh his second wife
Climbing up and down
the ladder of goodnights

Good night Getzl
Good night Shloymeleh
Good night Hayiml
Good night Frymeleh...

Good night Meereleh – my first first wife...

And then shuts his eyes
and raises his knees
To his chin
His hands clasped at the top
Of his head

Will he sleep?

What does he see
Behind his closed lids...?

Upon the Ridge

Upon the ridge of the galvanized sky
banked up snow
two stories high

Beneath a naked electric bulb
at the centre of a fly-specked
Ceiling

Traditional fly-
caravans bridge continents
of intour detour

Lou is growing wings
he studies the ceiling
And the iron bars

Also the long corridor with steel
doors and red lights
Moi Sheh Sheh Sheh
like the whisper of falling
October leaves

Ty jestesz jak zdrovie
You are like health
                zdrovie
                zdrovie
zdrovie that washed the cobbles
of my streets
mopped up blood
that couldn't be
mopped

I have mementos on shelves
in my Canadian home:
my Zaide's philacteries,
his undershirt with four
fringes a *Midrash* a *Zohar*
a Rambam, nigunym,[24]
an ivory pointer a silver
snuff box engraved by Uncle Yashke
with calligraphic letters:
Yoshke's *Reb Chiel Rebbe*
Chiel

I stood at the rear of Memme Chaye's
Panska courtyard upon the paving cobble
marked X on my Meeme's map
turning round and around
to get the feel of the half-forgotten
environs that brooded somewhere in the furthest
compartment of my overlaid memory with my
back to the wall against which the Germans
executed in 1916 Vlaczeslav Zieromski
the conductor of the Polish brass-band...

And I listen with cocked ear in
the hollowed space to his hoarse screaming
voice:
>   *"Niech zyje"*
>   *"Niech zyje"*
>   (Long live)
And then the salvo and puffs of
gray blue smoke of
six rifles

Grizzly memories marking time
press at the back of my eyeballs

Memeh Chaye

I see my meemeh dressed
in one of her very frilly
blouses clawing with her fingers fingernails
with an iron ladle and my meemeh Ruchl
her sister helping with a shining
new spade six eight cobbles steel
ladle and spade working together
setting aside six eight cobbles as replacements
enough space to fit the dimensions of the
strongbox with jewelry and time and
me to stand on twenty-three years later

While Sonia and Chave stand guard at the entrance
of the courtyard so as to signal that one
or two or many more are approaching
coming or going but no one came or went

There were steps of gendarmes or
soldiers or sailors passing on their way
to an Inn but nothing else
Only Pilka Sonia's little pup
came down the concrete staircase wagging its
tail, whimpering –

Six eight paving cobbles and then down
pressing the shoulder of the spade
with a foot and only lifting
four five ounces of dirt at a time and Meeme Ruchl
with an iron *tsulynt*-pot in her arms under the
loose-knit *vetshayle* leaving shining little
hills in four corners
and then the two of them
facing one another over the empty clay grave

lowering the strongbox to the bottom
replacing the freshly dug earth taking turns
and standing there with blue shadowed lips
staring into each other's eyes as into open graves
of time through a thousand years of Jewish
life in a mute *kaddish:*
>   *Isgadal ve'iskadash*
>   *Shmey rabo*[25]
>   And the timeless chant of:
>   SHEMA ISRAEL!
>   SHEMA ISRAEL!
>   SHEMA ISRAEL!

They then stamped down the earth
with their feet replaced the
cobbles and swept them dry into
the crevices and wept

I stood on the cobble marked
X on Meeme's courtyard map two
decades and years later in the
colours of an August sunset scanning
the windows of the courtyard wings
as the weaving windowpanes caught
fire in the golden
light
In sullen interior a painting
on a rear wall a part of a four post
bed a head of a horse on a pedestal
antlers on a wall part of a rocking-
horse, a panel of a credenza a corner
of a bare dining room table

And Meeme Chaye's second floor windows
with chintz curtains and the forms
of my mother, Meeme Chaye, Meeme
Ruchl three sisters behind the glass and the chintz
Standing together side by side at
this very window expropriated a long time ago
by a neighbour or someone high up in the
Polish regional government or an acclimated
German family with credentials and special
skills

The sisters' forms weave in my head
across the width of the casements/three spools
of winding thread in my father's textile
workshop whistling through
the Poznanski textile chimneys into a
spatial horizon above my Zaide's Polish
wood.

I stood with one foot on the X marked
cobble thinking thoughts that had little
to do with the strongbox of jewelry
when a small boy with a rucksack full
of books on his back and a schoolcap with
a shining visor over his eyes showed and there
there there I was/running through the
arch of the front entrance
and up the steps of the west wing
where Meeme Chaye stood waiting
for me on the concrete landing smiling down with
a brown bag of chocolate cookies extended in
both her hands

I looked at my wristwatch: it was four p.m.,

I was just a few minutes ago released
out of the second grade class-room of the
Hebrew gymnasium.

Meeme Chaye wore a *koleyke* necklace
of diamonds round her neck two silver
foxes flung over her shoulders diamonds
and rubies on three fingers of
each hand and Laye playing Schubert *lieder*
on the upright piano/Sonia with her
little curly gray-haired pup in arms and *Chaveleh*
dressed like a peacock with golden accessories
and high-heeled shoes that buttoned to the sides
into gold-stitched buttonholes doing
her homework at the wide window sill
in full regalia expecting
a prince, or a frog whom she could and would
turn into a prince a frog of frogs...

And my uncle Yashke on the high stool
at his workbench humming a new
Molly Picon song he had heard at the Scala
theatre/pottering with gold bars little
chisels a benzene blowtorch with a pure blue
flame out of a long nozzle and little
spoons of gold dipped in cups
and slivers of liquid solder
together with several sets of engraving tools
in velvet pouches and the metronome
    the metronome
    the metronome

"After... when this horrible war is over,"
Meeme Chaye wrote in the last letter a

letter in an envelope marked
with the same old return address
on Panska Lodz
she wrote, "I say prayers in my Yiddish
tchyneh prayer-book... If there is
a God in heaven, what is He doing there? Is He
deaf?
Blind?"

"I don't think anyone of us (us Jews
in Lodz) will survive..." it was as if she
were trying to communicate the uncommunicable
incomprehensible... "or anyone of us in Poland..."
"Yashke is in Budapest."
"Delivering commissioned items... Laye is
on a concert tour with a solo repertoire of
Chopin Brahms and Schubert..." Only one instant
behind the pride of a daughter's accomplish-
ment as if a thought was taking shape and
then dropped because it had turned into irrelevance
because of a greater vision of
wretchedness in the face of what? it seems
she understood and didn't understand or
understood and wouldn't couldn't believe
refused to understand couldn't believe her own conclusions of
doom sorrow beyond...
nightmare beyond distortion of thought
of language "What is happening to us?
What will become of us?"
and "The house is half empty... Just Esther
and Soniale and me..." and "Our sister Ruchl
is ailing... something wrong with two middle
fingers of her right hand... fester all the time
matter oozes through bandages.. the other
fingers seem to have lost colour of natural

skin and flesh... yellow-green and black
under fingernails... our local doctor Henryk
Myerovitsh says horror of horrors Cancer...
I am taking her to a famous doctor one Julian
Rakhlis in Varshe... just as soon as Yashke
returns from Budapest... I pray in *zechut*[26]
of our saintly father Reboyne-shel-Oylom
for help..." and "What will become of us?"

Meeme Chaye then relates the circumstance
of the burial of the strongbox with the
jewelry in the dark of a September night
immediately after the *Yom Kippur* fast...

"Velvl Kashtan the Balut blacksmith
put together a metal strongbox... Velvl is
nowadays the busiest Jew in Balut: strong-
boxes... for the burial of valuables... There
was a time when we could have run... now..."
and "the world closed in around
us feels like a suffocating prison with barbed walls
guns..." She sent regards from our
brother Layzer... "He is now working with
Yashke and will someday be a fine goldsmith...
Yashke has a lot of confidence in him complains
that Layzer works too many hours... I don't know
why..." that was the gist of the letter:
"I don't know why" the word "why" and the
feeling of foreboding... "Everything is at an end..."
and *es müss sein?*
the German *"es müss sein"* again
                              again
turned into a question "why *müss es sein!*"

"We already look like ghosts... the children
afraid fear themselves and one another and everyone
the Poles too are afraid of one another
even more than of the Germans... they get on
very well with the Germans seem to understand
the underlying mutuality of reasons: greed!!
loot... hate and fear, you can see it in their eyes...
complete absence
of sympathy or compassion
or even indifference they seem to say/
'you are through... doomed' and rubbing
their itchy palms together 'good riddance'..."

There was the enclosed map of the
courtyard on Panska with very precise instructions
...the pavement stone marked X on the map the distances
from the rear wall and the side wall a square
of three feet/one foot to the top of the
strongbox about twelve inches below the cobbled surface...

"if one of you gets back here after the war
he or she may lay claim to the strongbox and the
contents... Enclosed find authorization signed by
the three of us Yashke Ruchl and me..."
and "I am sending along a certified
copy so there will be no mistake... also a list of jewels, and
the rest?"

There was it seems a break
in the letter from what went before
a few days a week two weeks

Meeme Chaye continued from
where she left off:

"They the Germans or the Poles *(Adin Chort)*
can have the rest as long as
they leave us in peace..."

"I saw my Laye's grand piano
in Janek's Polish eyes...
he and Maciek Jablonski came to
ask after Yashke 'Where is he?
We haven't seen him around...'
'Out somewhere?' 'In the city?' 'Out of town?'
'Where out of town?'

They poked each other with elbows
in ribs in gesture of hilarity...
Some fun... *Psia krev do choroby...*[27]

"Janek turned his cap round and around
between the fingers of hands...
Jablonski seemed to
be on top of things/chief messenger
whatever the message... Maciek produced
out of his pocket an Ukaz or proclamation
"All Jews in this building must pack
one valise each and report to the
Rynek where the proper authorities will
receive them punctually at seven a.m.,"
and the final 'news':
"Failure of
appearance or registration is punishable
by death..."

How did she manage to post
this letter?

by what means? did she bribe one of the
Poles in the building? Whom? And
how did the letter get past the authorities
of the occupation? Aaaah, the postage stamp
said Bucharest Romania

Yashke... gets
around but how did it get into Yashke's hands
and why was Yashke now in Bucharest and not
in Hungary? The postal stamp showed
that the letter had been wandering
from hand to hand for the past three months
...a thought begins to form and suddenly
nothing... there are no longer any reasons
to think or speak or ask questions...
Or hope...!

After the war
the silence from Poland
shushed in my mind as I counted close
relatives close friends distant relatives
distant friends... humanized objects such
as pots remembered bits of particular
events a school desk a windowsill
the view outside the classroom window
a row of poplars and a little
further along a green painted fence an apple
tree an old lilac tree that sent scent
of sprouting lilac into the open window
in the spring of the passover and soon, soon
summer vacations

1 *Unvarstandlich* – Incomprehensible
  Varstandlich – Comprehensible (German)
2 *Draydl* – *Purym* top (Yiddish)
  Strulkes – agates (Yiddish)
3 *Gematria* – Kabbalist system of converting letters of
  Biblical texts into numbers
4 *Jerzelkes* – Midget pears (Polish)
5 *Shtille lieder* – Quiet songs (German)
6 *Esther ha'Malkah* – Queen Esther of *Purym* fame: married
  King Achashverot to save the Jewish community in Persia
  from total annihilation
7 *Sypurym* – Stories (Hebrew)
  Massioth – Stories (Hebrew)
  Mayselech – Little stories (Yiddish)
8 *Keepah* – Skullcap (Hebrew)
9 *Kretshmeh* – Tavern (Yiddish)
10 *Czynovnikes* – Gendarmes (Polish)
11 *Al Cheyt ... l'Foneycho* – For the sins committed against
   You (Hebrew)
12 *Chumysh* – Bible: Old Testament (Hebrew)
13 *Reboyne shel Oylom* – The Creator of the Universe
   (Hebrew)
14 *Baruch ha'Shem* – Blessed be His name (Hebrew)
15 *Lech l'cho* – Get going: God's order to Abraham (Hebrew)
16 *Ayns ... Fyyer* – One Two Three Four (Yiddish)
17 *Jak bylo tak bylo* – What was was (Polish)
18 *Harey zeh meshuboch* – The more shall He be praised
   (Hebrew)
19 *Zavierucha* – Snowstorm (Polish)
20 *Hakenkreuz* – Swastika (German)
21 *Es müss sein* – It must be (German)
22 *Na zdrovie* – To health (Polish)
23 *Shayne* – Pretty (Yiddish)

24 *Rambam* – Eleventh century philosopher, surgeon and
    theologian. He was the author of the book *Advice to the
    Perplexed.*
25 *Isgadal ... rabo* – Kaddish recited by mourners
26 *Zechut* – Prayer invoking the names of our ancestors:
    Abraham, Isaac and Jacob; or the name/s of ancestors
    deceased and now in Heaven
27 *Psia krev* – Hound's blood (Polish expletive)

FOUR

"There are three things
fitting for us:
Upright kneeling
Silent screaming
Motionless dancing."
                    – Rabbi Menachem-Mendl

My Father

My father came to me in a dream saying:
Everyone is waiting for you in Lodz.
Then: No one is waiting for you in Lodz.

In another dream I told him:
I am going there – immediately
                    immediately
                    immediately
He shook his head and walked slowly
into a dark-dead cloud. He muttered
from the other side of the cloud:
"Even when you were small you were
out of your head
out of your head
out of your head."

Hammering Down the Concrete Piles

I wait for the weave of
my nerves to steady and
subside

On Piotrkovska Street in Lodz
I saw a madman walk about
with an enameled chamber-pot
on his head

"Which," he said, "is only my
first limned act."

In my head partitions move about
on coasters as on the stage of the
Scala Theatre

To make room for seven
even blacker comedies

Gilded
sailboats on jade-green
fields of razor-sharp
tracks move hypnotically

In my recurrent dreams

Somewhere someone hammers a
nail into a brick wall
and then yanks it out with
Steel pliers to re-hammer
the same nail into another wall

Now all the walls
have nail holes

Somewhere black pile-drivers hammer
down concrete piles

Somewhere world-immigrants scream
out of inner nightmares on double
iron cots in this Detention House

Somewhere World-Immigrants scream
out of outer nightmares on upper
and lower iron cots in this Detention House

Somewhere Guards sleep in another time
a down-slope-time
a never-dream time
insomniac time

One by one in November light we
rush into Noah's waterproofed Ark

To face Noah's full-fledged *mahble*[1]

Flood flood flood
of velvet *Yeshiva yarmulkes*
afloat in the middle of an
emerald sea

Waiting for the unconsoled
carabineer

As a page in an open book with
special effects   turns into
an apocalyptic   carousel
in a waist-high   overexposed
haze of dry dust

Echoing footsteps in
hollowed corridors
reverberate in inner ears
against inner grain

Several Varieties of Schedule

My brother Layzer walks about
with

fingers in his
ears.

Doors on rusted hinges creak
and bang shut

On a rectangular
door-post an iron slab hammer-
on-anvil

unwound wound
in weave

The detention
of the eternal

I remember:
the first day in *Cheyder*[2]
my head was so bright
and hollow my compounding
eye pupils popped

I remember:
during the first day of
detention my brother Layzer
proclaimed:

"I need air."
and:
"I want to get out of this
place and breathe."

I told the nearest guard
about this
situation...

The guard pointed at a door
in a wall and said:
"Take him in there it's not
locked"

In the white-tiled lavatory
Layzer looked perpelexed wrong wrong
perspective... no sequence... he said:

"I've made up my mind I will
run away"

"Yes Layzer we will talk about it –
later"

Playing Ball in Reb Doovydl's Coal Yard

In afternoon September light
in random breeze of wind my mother's
brown-red curled head of hair
in our second-floor east-wing
window:
Moishe Moishe!!!
She leans out and across over
windowsill taking in/from
back to front/the expanse
of cobble pavement ranging
across over to the coal-shed roof where

My white goat's moth-eaten
head nods agreeably circling choices of
indifferent alternatives

Counting the wild hot-heads of
Jewish and Polish boys

The Psalm leaders[3]
of the sons of
Jacob and Esau

Dance in clouds of dust
with a *shmateh*[4] soccer-ball

Moishe Moishe!

Inaudible words
gurgle in dry throat ears
at sight of courtyard
prop

Chai and I saw the ladder
with the top rung in a
white cloud

No one else
No one else
No one else

The ladder in Beth-El shimmer
of climbing rungs

In perpetual motion
and yet at ease

Moishe Moishe!

Dumbfounded in the reserve
for the Elite hue of

Useless rhymes:
thus
      us
toss
ross
useless relevances
rolling up a lifetime of
boulders again and
again

What were Sisyphus's thoughts
on the way down?
          way down!

O send me your light
        your truth
        your truth
        your truth

Moishe Moishe!

The reality of the cast-iron
water-pump opposite Berl the
rope-maker's *varshtat*[6]

'Oo who will hang?
'oo who will swing?

Behind Nuhym the Dairy-man

Who will drink
Reb Nuhym's *shmeteneh.*[7]

Ahead of Shoolym the *Nafciarz's*[8]
gevelb[9]

What's that inside the arched rainbow
down the ladder's
descending rungs?

What's inside the brine barrel
of last summer's cucumbers
evaporate to level of
air

When my strength fails me
Forsake me forsake not/in some crossroad of
my paternal cantoral Zaide/recoursed

Al tashlicheynu
(do not forsake us.)

The cast-iron water-pump
opposite Berl the dairyman's flat
behind Nuhym the rope-maker
facing Shulym the Nafciarz
across Myer the soap-maker

And Sroolek the Nafciarz's twelve year old
son chants at the *sayfer* of
Boove Kamo

Maczek the Janitor sits on
his bench under the window of his
one-room flat with hands
between corduroyed knees

Matka Boska Matka Boska Matka Boska
(O mother of god)

Dozing in high fiesta time
Unapproachable in siesta time
except by regiments of
magnified
buzzing flies

"*Hasta basta
idziemy do miasta*
(we are going to town)

*Moishe Koisheh
Teekeh papier*"
(Oh it is high time
we went to the Market)

Thunderstruck wonderstruck
skip along
Chalk-marked square on
concrete pad

One foot here
one foot there
And Chai in blue crinoline
wants to be a butterfly...

My white goat Azazel
keeps score of the endless slight-
of-foot of our ball

If I had had a measuring-rod
if I had had a measuring-rod
I would have measured
the distances between the
central ladder of our
Beth-El courtyard
and the cast-iron waterpump

and the dairy-man
and the rope-maker
and the *Nafciarz*

and the soap-maker
and Shulym the Shoe-maker
with his apprentices
singing behind the mullioned
windows:

Shvester n'breeder
fyn arbet n'noit

Mir alleh vus zenen
cezayt n'ceshprait[10]

If I had had
if I had had

the zeal for Thy House that
hath eaten us up

"And behold a wall on the outside
of the house round about and in
the man's hand a measuring rod
of six cubits long of a
cubit and a hand breadth each
So he measured the breadth of the
building one reed wide and the
height one reed

"Then came he unto the gate which
looketh toward the East and went up
the steps thereof and he measured the
jamb of the gate one reed broad
and the other jamb one reed broad and
every cell was one reed long."[11]
High   cool

And down the second floor window
my mother *Dveyreh,* face down

Moishe, Moishe!

The decisive soccer game
progresses: messages of raised eyebrows
signals from mouth to mouth eye-to-eye

Everyone except Loozer is covered
with sweat from head to foot

Loozer barks penalties
voice tinged with melancholia... commands...
points to the waiting bench left
right forwards raises his voice to
a pitch when the ball
hovers close to Nootl's
goal

One lone forward/Stasz/kicks the
ball past Nootl as Nootl swallows
a mouthful of dust

Moishe Moishe!

Horses bray
on a distant planet
What happened up there
in the house?

Father fell ill/nausea again/Brantsheh
Or Tzypl are ill/
Must run this minute to
Jablonski the *Feldsher*[12]

bring him to the house
with satchel full of
glass *bankes*

Or: a letter arrived from
Beyrysh and Mechl...

Or: Beyrysh came home
Or: Mechl came home
Or: Beyrysh and Mechl
came home...
came home...

Mother's Kinder Yurn[13]

Kinder yurn mayne shayne blumen[14]
children clap hands prefer:
Patsh-patshe-kyichelekh[15]

Mother's unfinished Yiddish
novel drenched in heartbreak
abandoned somewhere on a
kitchen shelf in our first
Canadian house on Oxford Street
in Toronto

(Rent: thirty dollars a month –
in 1927)

Title of unfinished novel:
If I Had Wings If we had wings...
Father said: "It is not impossible...
Nooo kon zayn"[17]
In iridescence

In the fleece of churned sleep
rubbing his eyes
with knuckles

Mother reading Shakespeare line by line
in light of kitchen window
at *Serateh*-covered[18] kitchen-table
as night visions turn into
wings by the skin of their teeth

"If" Rebbe Alimeylekhs feet
did not grow stone-heavy
he would have danced
with the trees
on a floor of oak needles and acorns
in fervent praise of gathering-clouds

Kinder Yurn mayne shayne blumen

As I remember I see a tiger
crouch between taut lines

In a cage behind bars of
terror only six feet
long by measured steps of feet

Mother's quaint folk songs
still rock me to sleep
on the runners of my cradle
in Lodz

Her words stand before me
in order and without
constraint in mirror

Kinder kinder kinder

Driven by light into darkness
and run out of this unfazed
world

Into the dark chamber of the mournful
chapel before the
king of terror of
silence

O childhood years
my precious
golden angels in full flight
as the winds pass

O where were you when
I laid the foundations of the
earth?

When I was three I came down with brain fever
through bright light sunbeams in the
sky looping unlooping

I balanced the seas along the waves
reversed the balance of
clouds talked out of a burning bush
that could not consume me...

rescued wild ghosts
from up stony ledges
of mountains
harnessed six wild
horses to my fiery
chariot

And mother ran to fetch
the Surgeon general of the
German occupation army
in the year 1915

She went down to her knees and
kissed his shining leather boots

Begging in the name of the
ordinances in heaven layer upon layer –
for help

The German doctor clicked his heels
bowed and raised my mother to her feet

The German doctor unharnessed all my wild horses,
brought me down from the
peaks of mountain-sheafs of dust
scattered my wild goats
drew the curtains and draperies
together so I could change my mind and lay down my sword
and rest

O the childhood years
will not return
not even in the fleece
of my dreams

Mother walked across the kitchen
and through the rear door into
her rhubarb garden as I
put out the lamp above my head
so I could talk to her when she
returns in the dark

Yashkeh-Maryshkeh

And:
"Yashkeh Maryshkeh vus hostu gemacht
ekh byn nysht geshloofn
a gantse nakht."[19]

"I stayed awake all night?"
"I didn't sleep all night."

O riddle me riddles
paradox me paradoxes
of collapsing oaks
in my Zaide's wood

Riddled woodsmen
inside terror-wood
dreadful sound of
felled oaks

I am in a circus ring
talking to lions and tigers
about African mountains

Listening to mother's shuttle tales of fish
of horseraddish and ancient elixirs

Colour of Midrash heroes
waiting for the Messiah

Father:
The Messiah will arrive on a wild ass
when not one of us will need him

O kinder yurn
mayne
ahaym gegangen alleh
gezoogt a giteh macht[20]

They all went home and
said goodnight
said goodnight
said goodnight

Rayzeleh dem Shoikhet's
was beautiful beyond words
Yashkeh Maryshkeh vus hostu gemacht
And when Rebbeh Alimelech needed
the merry *Klezmers*
he sent his *Shamys*[21]
to fetch them

Echoing footsteps
heavy doors on squeaking hinges
bang shut

The pile-drivers are hammering
down the concrete piles
down the concrete piles

My brother Layzer sits up on
his iron bunk in the Canadian Detention house in Halifax

with fingers in
both his ears

The sluggard says:
there is a tiger outside
come out of the illustrated pages

"I shall be slain in the streets
We will be slain in the streets

By the potentate against whom there
is no uprising..."
By the potentate against whom we shall rise

In the morning when the
sun rises a golden rooster
rises to keep its oath
saying: Kukurehhhkuuu
I am one and whole fully alive
        kukurehhhkuuu
in shrine upon ridge
of perch in the upper world
            with blood red comb
            kukerrruuukoooo

And those who seek blindness
stare at the sun
those who bounce off head
the soccer ball
in wrong direction...

grope in circle
without light...

I see part of the ceiling
above and beyond mother's
head

On the ceiling a zigzag zagging crack
in the white plaster like an
inscribed raddish-nose

And a shorter crack and two
oval grief-smitten eyes
showing stripes of yellow
plaster-lath

Along an all-harm cradle
in an all-harm pepper cradle

Grinning down at me from ceiling
in framed window
an astonished head of
          blind madness

I had
a football between my feet
(ran with it to eternity
rolled over (against interdiction)
riding the warm wind in and out
                        out of openings
from one foot to another
inner and outer against an opposite
forward centre player named Voitek the
Vidzever/in goal-passage

Side by side dancing to haunting deafening
tune side-stepping "O you
big Vidzever Ham." wider
and shorter mugged by coal-dust
more than ex-pec-
ted.

Laughing up sleeve Ha ha ha
charred mug ech oh it comes
up to zero zeroing in

Voitek in my ear:
"I'll take what you got
I'll kick your balls
high and wide
do Palestyny!"[22]

Moishe Moishe!

What? (Vuys?)

Mir Furn Ka Kanadeh

Voitek kicks the ball
from between my feet
het het in the opposite
ech direction where little Nootl
our goal keeper
chews a lemon to
cure his squeamish stomach

Moishe Moishe!

"What? What!"

"*Mir furn ka Kanadeh...*"
"*ka vyi?*"
"*ka Kanadeh*"23

Who shall be saved who shall perish
one day, soon...

"Right this minute?"
"*Mir furn mir furn.*"

"He that keepeth the peace is like
an eagle that flies over the
mountain over a valley
of a dead city."

All windows open at once
antique heads appear from
between chintz curtains

Reb Hersh walks arthritically across
the courtyard with his white beard

over his shoulder like a
flag of surrender
"where is it Dveyrele?"

Arybern Yam.[24]

An empty tin can kicked aside
a *sheheyonu* in the window
of cancer-eaten Naftuly

Sroolek the Nafciarz's son
chants in his high-squeaky voice
a blat of *Booveh Kamoh*

Chaml on the subtstitute-bench
along the coal scale
memorizes a Tshernichovski poem

Loozer in his determinate-indeterminate
space of percolating time
pokes a sharp elbow in my ribs
a bland unfinished grin round the corners
of his mouth

"O Moishe you've been replaced
my friend."

"What?"
"Ever read *Siddhartha* Moisheleh?"
"What?"
"Now tell me the truth Moishl can
you read?"
"Read what?"

It was recess time
Loozer has lots of time

140

His father fumbles at the scales
weighing sacks of coal Chaml on the
bench already got his signal he was
on/
He stops in the middle of
a stanza and runs to
take my place

Still Loozer pursues pedantically:

"Ka na deh? Why Ka na deh *noo! noo...*
folg mech a gang.[26]
Why not to Australia Japan Africa
or China ha ha ha kana dadoo."

At that very moment
all threads on father's looms
in his shop
broke at once

Dye powder seeped down
through his fingers

Perforated white clouds
above the monumental Beth El
ladder turned
into black
elephants

Thunder thudded in my heart

Thunder and lightning shook the
earth at once –

God accepted Abel's gift
and rejected Cain's

God smoked soap bubbles
through a heavenly straw

Abel had chosen the best lambs of
his flock carrying them in
both arms against his chest

Cain had set a few flax seeds
upon the stone altar

Moreover
he answered god's rebuke ("is that
all you could spare?")
With a cry that is still
echoed by the blasphemers round
every corner:
"THERE IS NO LAW AND NO JUDGE."

Someone breathed poison into the blades of a hurricane

Meeting Abel in a field afterwards
Cain complained brother-to-brother:

"There is no world to come
"No heaven and no hell

"No reward for the righteous
no punishment for the sinners

"This world/Abel/was not
created in mercy –

Neither is it ruled in
compassion"

Abel said: "You know all that?
since when?"

Cain said:

"Why else has your offering
been accepted and mine
rejected?"

Abel said:

Mine were accepted because I love God
yours was rejected because you hate him."

Cain then (in a fit of rage)
struck Abel and killed him

We walked down the concrete staircase
across the courtyard through the
archway of the entrance into the
cobbled street toward the railway track
and the crossroads

A hundred roosters began their
Kukurehhhkuuu prayers
to the sun

A hundred roosters perched
upon the broken gables of
the green gold acacia trees

143

Loozer blew his whistle
on an infraction
when lightning
struck

The soccer game between us
and the Vidzever
hooligans came to a draw

Birds sang to one another
on scorched branches
about ancestral
ghosts in holy holy holy light

One week later when we won
(six to one) there was a
pogrom

I saw a black crow in the flame
of a candle in the half-dream
of a nightmare

1   *Mahble* – Flood (Yiddish)
2   *Cheyder* – (Literally: 'room' in Hebrew) Primary one-room school in Yiddish and Hebrew
3   *Psalmists* – King David's psalms
4   *Shmate* – Rag (Yiddish)
6   *Varshtat* – Workroom (Yiddish)
7   *Shmeteneh* – Sour milk (Yiddish)
8   *Nafciarz* – Lamp-oil salesman (Yiddish)
9   *Gevelb* – Shop or store (Yiddish)
10 *Shvester ... ceshprait* – Sisters and brothers / of toil and pain / all of us scattered / and lost in this world (Yiddish song of protest)
11 *Ezekiel* – 40:6 (Hebrew)
12 *Feldsher* – Barber; also medic (Yiddish)
13 *Kinder yurn* – Childhood years (Yiddish)
14 *Kinder ... blumen* – Childhood years, my pretty flowers (Yiddish)
15 *Patsheh* – Clap hands (Yiddish children chant)
17 *Kon zayn* – May be (Yiddish)
18 *Serateh* – Oil cloth (Yiddish)
19 *Yashke ... nacht* – Yashke Maryshke what did you do? We haven't slept all night.
20 *Ahaym ... nacht* – They said goodnight and left for home. (Yiddish)
21 *Shumys* – Beedle (Yiddish)
22 *Do Palestyny* – Go to Palestine (Polish)
23 *Kanadeh* – Canada
24 *Arybern yam* – Over the ocean (Yiddish)
26 *Fold mech a gang* – What a walk (Yiddish)

FIVE

"Who knows the length of time
when night lowers the curtain
on what is happening in its
depth" — Bruno Shultz
        from *Sanatorium Under the Sign
        of the Hourglass*

Positive and Negative Trends

My Zaide Chyiel Reb Yoske's
once walked from Pruskove to
Varshe on a Sabbath day[1]
to intervene in the sentencing
of two young Jewish Bundists
to prison or worse

We lived in these
Lodzer streets in the green light
under myrtle/during the
Succoth days we partook in
blessings and meals
songs and wine
with one another
in peace – reading letters
          from Chamitzchyk Chamitzchyk
          from Toronto Canada

One black cloud sets out to meet the
other the other is more interesting
than the one with breath-clouded
glass in hand

The other hugs the great book
of grief with blue flaps
and blue tail in the wind

Choosing appropriate segments of
available space on this grounded side

But no cloud rose to stand
or sit to rest as people
sit to rest at table

Father danced two-stepping to tune
of a *Gerer neegn*[2]
between the cubits of the
Zawadzka street workshop —

Round and around his magic drums
of textile dye with
inner scarlet face and green
raised veins in momentary warp/
cape over shoulder a camera
with a faulty lens out of focus
thereof a woodchuck smile in
Zaide's wood

In My Mother's Stove

In mother's stove Reb Doovydl's
dust coal brickettes turn to ash

Memories rose amiably
and halted before burnt offerings
at the rim of rubble

Outworn rubbled speeches come apart
at the joints

Here and now nobody answers to the names
of my memory/except trees street lanterns
houses running into the fire
in Balut

My white goat lowered his head
and I grabbed his teak horns

*"Yntern kind's viegeleh zitst
a vays vays tsiegeleh."*[2A]

He pushed
I pushed

*Der tateh yz avek handlen
myt roxshynkes n'mandlen*[3]

The goat soon pinned me to the
coalyard fence and looked
up:

"Take back your goddam sins
you patched up son of Cain!!!"

In nip and tuck
at the rim of rubble

The last letter from Nootl
dated February 1942 from
Balut Lodz forwarded to me
from Toronto to the airforce barracks
in Skuduck:

    "Moishe Moishe Moishe?
    Wus Machstu?[4]

    Du yn Balyt ys bloyz TOYT[5]
    ("Here is only DEATH")

Frost on
stone cobble pavement frost on
green moss and limestone coping/of
parapets down riddled walls

Zymund's naked torso/visible high up
on the roof/whistles in
with two fingers in mouth
yet one more pigeon flock

Herr Shultz

Herr Shultz stands in the middle
of the courtyard to the right side
of the central ladder measuring
with bleary eyes a lemon-coloured
world in alcohol haze – athwart

Measuring inverted rote
from Lodz
to Berlin's
Alexanderplatz

Herr Shultz with cane like a rifle
over hunched shoulder

A formidably shaken cavalryman
without saddle or horse –

And Nootl dressed
in a green oversize hand-knitted sweater
and a stocking-cap looks at
Herr Shultz quizically
as if to say:
"*Folg mech a gang...*"

And "*Ech*" and "*Ot azoy*" and[6]
"Thus and thus..." *ze* and *ze*
and:
"*Noch a meshugener...*"[7]
"Another crazy..." "*Adin chort...*"[8]

Fables take shape in Nootl's head
follow a swan goose with an orange
beak and trot out of the

ranged caves in the back
of head/like spider
on hammock of cobweb

A nymph out of a *mykveh*[9]
on a marvellous night like this
speaks four-letter words
out of a clenched heart

God suffuses the sun
drowns an Egyptian army
you can still see the white
helmets on boisterous waves
of the Red Sea

And from here on
the past is the future
the future the past
Along the dry path
of the parted sea

In the greying evening
Herr Shultz turns into a field
Marshall:

"*Nicht zurück drehen!*"[10]
and:
"*Ihm Widerstand!*"[11]

Cobbles pavement like an army
of cobbled heads

A lost tune out of
a music-grinder's black box
with a popinjay fortune-teller

ground out by a
blonde Pole with soft oyster eyes
and a peculiarly unhinged arm

Diabetes-scurvy-and-cholera *mechitza-*
tunes of the end of days

and Herr Shultz circles
wobbledy round the
central courtyard ladder:

Herr Shultz:
"*Heraus donnervetter*
heraus donnervetter!"

("Goddamit out out!
into lightning
thunder!")

Our House According to Ezekiel

And there were windows and doors
within the four inner four square walls
and in each corner of the courtyard
there was a sparse acacia tree – perhaps

And the windows and doors and architraves
and upper copings and the iron balconies
thereof faced the inner courtyard – almost

And the going up into
the chambers was by
wide concrete steps
and square concrete landings
at each half flight at the
exact centre of each wing
eastward and northward and
westward

And the southward wing
was a courtyard-wide
high green fence which was
a *Mechitzah*[12] between
the inner courtyard and the
coal-yard with its flat
tar-covered roofs corresponding
in length to the length of the
coal-yard and in width to the
width of a commodious
coach-and-horse eight
yards deep by measuring rod
more or less

And I did in the long ago measure
the widths lengths heights thereof
and the arched inner courtyard entrance
between the two walls leading into
the inner courtyard and the entrances
to the lower and upper chambers
at the centre of each wall

and up the first flight (eight steps) to
the first concrete square landing with its
outer cantilevered iron balcony and then
up the second flight
of concrete stairs (again eight steps)
to the second landing which led on
one side to Chaml Myerson
the head bookkeeper of Poznanski's
textile factories (with a family of six
two daughters and two grown sons)
on the one side and our own chambers
on the right side

And the chambers of Reb Hersh
of Rashi fame with his wife Sooreh and
his son Gershn and daughter Ryfkeh
and Reb Doovydl the coal man with his
wife Bleemeh and son Loozer and
Reb Gedalyeh the watchmaker
a family of eleven three daughters and
six grown sons and up higher
Menahym Rozenberg the
Bookbinder a family of eight
three sons and three daughters

"Did you hear?"
"what?"
"Pan Jozef Pilsudski is dead."[13]

Scuffs and scratches on Nootl
the goal-keeper's knees
palms of hands
coal-black
character-language
of
expression when Nootl
rages against Loozer the
referee.

"What about Pilsudski? Is he
really dead?"
"When they say he is dead he is dead."

"So what will they do with his
sleepwalking white horse?
And what will we do?
Say *Kaddish?*"

Bolt of lightning cuts colliding
clouds in shreds like silver thread

"How awful!" Chai laments
Nootl shrugs:
"I wouldn't call it awful... You
better apologize..."
"Apologize?"
"in a way..."

The Facades

The facades of the buildings
on the way to Balut
Don't match

the courtyards
lean and mourn
one prays another blasphemes
some things about them are bad
others worse... in opening path...

My right hand is estranged from
my left they no longer
clasp hands with one another
behind my back
behind my back

An old blind man leans on my arm
as I guide him on Piotrkovska
Ulitsa across the road

He talks staring straight ahead
out of blindness I can not
understand a word he says he
has only one brown tooth in his black
mouth
he says *"Dupa jasna pizda czasna"*[14]
only the words run together – slurred

In a first floor window on Zavadska Ulitsa
I see a blonde woman's emaciated face
eyes large and staring out of
yellow pouches

her name is Bleemah-Ruchl
her name is Panna Jadviga, name is Bleemah

My cab driver
a stern Pole with a red-and-purple nose
tells me that Panna Jadviga is
Po trochu potrochu[15]
Dying of cancer

I am in a one-horse *droshka*
The driver doesn't
use his whip the whip is
at his right side in a tubular
casing he only uses his *laitzes*[16]

Where am I going?
I don't know
Why am I here in this city?
                in this city?
                in this city?

The Year We Left Poland

The year we left Poland
my uncle Yashke went to
Budapest then Bucharest
then Jerusalem

We have letters somewhere to
that effect he says he is true
to his name "*Yashke furt...*"[17]
he talks about plans:

To see the world "before it blows
up in my face..." he had
attended a philharmonic concert
where "my Layeleh performed
on the piano to a packed hall..." "She was
so beautiful and precious I cried
couldn't stop crying all night...

I am seeing her tomorrow morning
for breakfast and lunch... at her
hotel..."

When Yashke left my Meemeh Ruchl the *almooneh*[18]
moved in with meemeh Chaye on Panska Street

Meemeh Chaye wrote to say that she misses
Yashke something terrible "He is and
always will be a *grossartiker Meshugener*[19]
but I keep seeing him in his backroom *varshtat/*
singing the *kiddush* at the head
of the table/bowing right
and left in the scala reserved box
as if he were the main attraction...

and dancing from room to room with Layeleh
Sonya and Chaveleh..." And "Oy oy ay ay ayvay."

"My heart weeps: *Yashke yz avek...*"
she wrote: "The house is full/two
old mothers waiting for weddings and
grandchildren and six growing grown daughters..."

She wrote: "Layeleh is on a circuit tour
she will perform in Budapest Bucharest, Vienna
Amsterdam Paris and Rome... Then in Varshe
and Lodz it will take a full season before
we will see her again... we miss her.

"Sonya graduated with full honours from
the Gymnazium she is preparing to leave
for a Kibbutz somehwere on the Galilee Sea
...maybe it's for the better... I don't know
only the *Oybershter*[20]... knows.

"There is a lot of merriment singing and
deviltry in the house... Ruchl is busy cooking
and reading *Tchyneh*[21] Ruchl's elder
daughter Dina is attending a university
in Vienna she is studying Economics/why?/
I don't know... what good will economics
do her? I don't know/she writes twice a
week but no engagement no marriage...

"There is much merriment in the house
singing and laughter quarrels and re-
conciliations the girls dance from
mirror to mirror young men knock
on the door with flowers boxes of choco-
lates but nothing... I am waiting impatiently
Ruchl is waiting impatiently... and no

Yashke... Yashke... my heart aches
morning noon and night... there is someone
at the door I must run...”

My legs are too short why are my legs too
short? I already inquired
there is nothing I can do about it
they are not stretchable but then
Nootl's legs are even shorter

In Meemeh Chaye and Yashke's courtyard
on Panska I heard Layeleh
practicing the
scales on the Heintzman grand piano
unlimited contrary combinations of hesitant
playfulness

In the inner courtyard the windowsills
and copings are yellowed limestone fa-
cades with architectural ornamentations
that have long since been abandoned
(due to the cost of skilled labour materials
and the *sky-scraping* minimalists)

In My Memory – Roman Numericals

High and wide windows with carved keystones
windows lined with velvet flutes of drapes and
portières/in the apartment the predominant
long walnut dining-table with high-backed
carved chairs to match/suddenly
peopled with ghosts of my family discussing
over a Friday night Sabbath meal Emma Goldman
Chayim Weitzman a book of poems by the young
Julian Tuvym a Morris Szwartz play in the
Scala Theatre...

In my memory accommodating shadows
move from moment to moment in the
windows between velvet drapes
coloured leaves on treebranches like
bits of scarlet paper/ a thin
woman across the court stares into
space/and how terrible to be thinking
of Layeleh in Auschwitz walking through
shadows of absence up dull-lit
stairs towards her winged piano to thunderous
applause then suddenly shrinking shrieking
emptying herself
of emptiness

And the massive Biedermeier furniture my
uncle imported from Berlin or Vienna
together with the glass-fronted china
cabinet

with fine miniature pieces of
sculptures/Chinese jade African ivory Prague crystal
and little wonder-figures brought from travels

in Africa in my uncle's brown cowhide
satchel

And a wedding portrait of Yashke and Chaye
in a polished wood oval frame/Yashke with a
wayward gleam in eyes dressed in gabardine tails
Chaye in wedding gown of lace
staring wistfully into space

On the opposite wall a
Chagall of groom-and-bride flying into
a private Eden over Vitebsk roofs

Stanislav the ancient toothless janitor
is still at his post in the basement
I see him now as he creaks across
the cobbled pavement of the inner court towards
the arched front entrance with a ring of
heavy keys in arthritic hand

And I suddenly locate the old oak tree against
the blind brick fence with its
annual crop of acorns

And Chinese Persian and Pakistani
throw rugs on the highly waxed
intricately patterned parquet floors/and
paper angels with cardboard noses

Stanislav's wife Vrurzkah hunched over
sweeping with cornbroom in clawed hands
the courtyard cobbles:
Today all the yesterdays and
only god knows about the tomorrows...
only god knows about the tomorrows...

And Stanislav beckoning a small boy (me)
with a rucksack of books over his shoulders
to show him with pointer in hand
a graphic personal nightmare along
the rear brick fence

As I in my mind climb in a beam of blue
light the concrete stairs to see if
the woman across the courtyard with the sunken
cheeks and vacant eyes still stares in her window
into our space

I remember in gas light glow a diamond
Koleikeh framed in white
gold on golden chain round Meemeh
Chaye's pale tall neck/light fused
to third dimension (fashioned in Yashke's
varshtat) down the cleft
between pale breasts a miniature elephant-
ivory temple/a silver
mink jacket twin silver foxes
with black-shoe-button eyes/velvet and
damask bustled gown

gold from monazite red garnet from zircon
platinum sifted from chromate windows as sheer
as air

and the wall tapestries my uncle brought back
from Abyssinia/
ceiling-high glass-front locked
bookcases showing gold embossed leather
jackets

And strange strange strange to
remember after so much time to feel the

same feelings even stronger
after so many years have settled

On the inner windowsills/in my
Meemeh's house there are boxes of
crayons, boxes of coloured pencils
exercise books/serialized
Three Musketeers/Arabia Magic
Monte Cristo Pan Tadeusz Quo Vadis

On the heavy teak credenza alongside
a silver *Menorah* are Yashke's six
mershaums[22] A shard of blue glass
an oval Russian egg, a porcelain windmill an
abstractness of a dadaist vision

Niech Zyje[23]

Stanislav the coshmar of a creaking janitor
points at the bullet holes
in the rear brick wall

As soon as the Germans arrived
they arrested forty Polish
musicians of the local brass-band and
executed them against this wall
four at a time... "for playing
the National Anthem *O jescze*
Polska nie zginela nie zginela
boom boom dadadadahhh zginela

Our Poland will live
as long as our hearts beat... still.

Stanislav painted the scene with his quaver
panting/gasping
for air and shaking his head

The soldiers with the rifles against
shoulder trigger fingers on triggers
staring down the sights
towards the condemned men without
blindfolds shouting
    niech zyje niech zyje niech zyje[23]

One by one and one on one

The Poles fell forward on their faces
and then rose to be shot again
and then rose again
to be shot again

In Stanislav's old head

Behind my back the facades
of the buildings don't match

Neither do the inner courtyards on the way
to Balut...

1   *Varshe* – Warsau (Yiddish)
2   *Gerrer nign* – A Gerrer Rebbe tune (Hebrew)
2   A *Yntern ... tsigeleh* – Beneath your crib sleeps a white kid (Yiddish)
3   *Der Tateh ... mandlen* – Your father is away dealing with raisins and almonds (Yiddish)
4   *Vus machstu* – How are you (Yiddish)
5   *Du yz ... Toit* – Here in Balut there is only death
6   *Ot azoy* – Thus (Yiddish)
7   *Noch a Meshugener* – Another crazy (Hebrew)
8   *Adin chort* – The same blundering devil (Russian)
9   *Mykveh* – Ritual bath (Hebrew)
10 *Nicht zurück drehen* – No turning back (German)
11 *Ihm Vidershtand* – Counter-attack (German)
12 *Mechitzah* – Division (Hebrew)
13 *Pilsudsky Jozef* – Army officer and President of the Polish Republic after the First World War (1867-1935)
14 *Dupa ... czasna* – Bright ass tight cunt (Polish)
15 *Potrochu potrochu* – Bit by bit (Polish)
16 *Laitzes* – Reins (Yiddish)
17 *Yashke furt avek* – Yashke is going away (Yiddish)
18 *Almuneh* – Widow (Yiddish)
19 *Grosartiker Meshugener* – First-class crazy (Yiddish)
20 *Oybershter* – Allmighty (Yiddish)
21 *Tchyneh* – Prayer-books in Yiddish translated from Hebrew
22 *Mershaum* – Pipe (Yiddish)
23 *Niech zyje* – Long live (Polish)

SIX

My memory stands in the dark mirror
inside a hurricane of
images

A Few Stars Came Out

My Zaide's *midrash* has many
honest and wicked tales

wrapped in all colours
gliding under
over like my father's
skeins of thread dipped
in dye

In his stained hands

My zaide intones:
When Rhab Saphra once
sailed on a ship
rocking on waves he saw a two-horned
beast lifting its head
out of the water

As Rhab Saphra held his breath
he saw engraved on the beast's
horns the terror-words:
"*this tiny creature measuring
two hundred leagues is on its
way to serve as Leviathan food.*"

The Chalcese are a substitute
for the Ichneumon (no bigger
than a small dog some say
a herring or a sprat) But even
the Behemoth which roved
the heights of a thousand mountains
feared the Ichneumons

because they
dug for bones
where there were none...

The courtyard fortune-teller
tells me: Demolish all
your zigzagged dreams...

you say you drowned a whale
a whale never 'drowns' in other
words: make sense
even when you are dreaming.

When I returned to my green bench
in my Kolye Gurtn in Lodz
an old woman in a faded
green overcoat told me
from across the other end of the
bench that her oldest son
the Viennese doctor wears
wire-rimmed eyeglasses and
talks into an earth-black tube in the language of
saints.

She had green eyes gray wrinkled
cheeks an upturned nose and a green
fairy-tale tongue

I did what Chai wanted
me to do!
preliminary-beginnings –
Isotope of Rhodon in elements of
                              light

We held hands
we listened to one another's heart
we felt each other's knees elbows

I could hear her hinged bones
in the knees and elbows grow

She could not hear my knees
and elbows grow

Now fifty-nine years later
I try to remember
the sound of her growing bones

I tremble when my knees
turn to water

I stutter when I try to
tell her   everything
                 everything
                 everything

Now everything is subordinate to
nothing   nothing

I try to remember why I stuttered

Chai explored my mouth teeth
gums tongue with her sticky lollipop
fingers

Sweeter than Meeme Chaye's
little chocolate
Kiehelech[1]

In a world with accessible
mountains made of
raisins
and almonds   and almonds

The Book of Aziel

My zaide said:
King Solomon is said to have
won much of his wisdom
from the 'Book of Aziel'
which was a collection of
Astrological Secrets
cut in saphire

According to the Slavonic Book
of Enoch it was Yahweh who
wrote the Book of Aziel

It was also Yahweh
who appointed two angels:
Samuil and Raguil
to accompany Enoch
back from Heaven to Earth

He commanded Enoch to give
the Book to his children and children's
children

According to Jewish mythology
the Book of secret wisdom was
given to *Oodym ha'ryshon*[2]
from whom it descended
through Noah Abraham Jacob Levi
Moses Joshua until it reached
King Solomon

The legend says that each and
every day the angel Aziel stands

upon Mount Horeb and proclaims
the book's secrets to all mankind

His voice reverberates
around the world

— according to Targum on
Ecclesiastes 10:20

I wrote "reverberate" on a page of
papyrus on the windowsill
of the Halifax Detention House

But the letters blotted
the words ran away and melted
in the snow

There is only one little line
that remains out of my
brouhaha addenda:

Let's go and play in the
other room
other room.

What other room?
What's in the other room?

Ocean waves still shimmer
in transparency as I write:
"emerald green with grayhead
whitecaps"
across from end to end

I tried to get into the
other room but the other room
was a long empty corridor

A guard who left the door unlocked
barked me back into the
room with the iron cots
        with the iron cots

The Ziz

My zaide recalls that
Bar Hana
and his shipmates on an ocean voyage
once saw a *Ziz*[3] standing in
mid-ocean –
the waves wetted
only
his
ankles

Bar Hana writes:

"We judged that the sea must be shallow
and thought to disembark and cool
ourselves but a heavenly voice
warned us: 'Seven years ago
a ship's carpenter dropped his axe
at –
this spot
and it has not yet
reached bottom.'"

This is the story of *Bird Ziz*
                    of *Bird Ziz:*

"Though taking good care of
her huge eggs and
hatching them on a far-off mountain
on the ledge of a rock she
eventually let an addled
one fall...

the stinking
contents of the addled egg
drowned sixty Cities and
swept away three hundred cedar
trees..."
(B. Bekhorot 57:B)

In the park above my
bench under raining tree –
tears ran down
Kosciuszko's[4] face

Why is he crying?

Is he perhaps trying to
restore the mystery of the
nightmare of the American Revolution?

Down the concrete stairs
past the iron balcony
across the courtyard
through the covered archway

We sat on the green bench
holding hands

Above us Kosciuszko's eyes and the leaves
ran down with no-stop tears

Enough to drown two and a half
Polskie Woisko[5] khaki brigades

Testing tasting testing tasting
the gritty soot the circle of galloping pain
of alter life –

on the slaughter
fields

I tried to tell Chai everything

Instead I told her that I
intended to leave home
to join a Galilee Kibbutz

She said:

"When?"
I said:
"As soon as I finish my eighth grade."

I stood
with one foot forward and one hand
pointing the way like Adam

Mickievicz[6] in Varshe on the shores
of the *Visla*[7]

*Oz tus ha'Hyrayon ke'Ketzef
al mayim*[8]

There was no blue iron train
there was no blue iron train
there was no stone staircase
there was no silver bridge

I just tried to tell Chai
everything

Chai was busy twining a twist
of a hundred and eighty-five

yellow dandelions into a
golden crown
for her head

Drops of rain on
awning rod hesitate
reflecting parts of heavenly roughing
light

Pollen-stained wide-eyed children sing:

*Alef Bays Gyml Dalyd
Hai Vuv Zoyim Ches
Tes*

Deafening the principalities of heaven

Yideleh a careful little Jew rests
on a stone slab
in full regalia of tassled undergarment
and prayer-shawl: on the way
to *Yerusholayim* in vernacular

Reb Hersh   folding one leg
                 over the other
                 with both hands
Head tilted to the side
of left shoulder
eyelids down:

"When Moses threw the magic wand
into the red sea the waters
contrary to the expected miracle
did not divide to leave dry
passage for the chosen people."

Hersh then sighs and lifts the folded
leg off the leg beneath
And the leg beneath
over the leg that had been
on top

Noo Azoy

"*Noo azoy azoy azoy* (thus) thus the waters
did not divide until the first man
jumped in!"..

A sparrow flies under the ceiling
among the hot-water pipes of the
Detention House in Halifax

A dead sparrow fell from a water pipe
onto my cot

Will Layzer stop crying when
it stops snowing???
Will it
stop snowing?
Will Layzer stop crying?

when it stops snowing
we will still be here
wishing to be somewhere else

Layzer
watches the snow and the road
below

He watches a squirrel with
paws at mouth
on a naked branch of a winter tree

There are plenty of
frozen chestnuts in the
snow

Reb Hersh with both feet on the
floor inserts a pinch of
snuff into each nostril and then
uppehtshuuuuh three times and
then: straightening in his seat:
"When Rabbi Menachem Mendl of
Vorki was once asked what
constitutes a good Jew
he said: *Three things are
fitting for us:*   *upright kneeling*
                          silent screaming
                          motionless dance."

In Meemeh Chaye's house the yellow-green
canary refused to sing

"Noo," Uncle Yashke said to the bird
"let's hear something a little tune a
peep, anything!"

The bird swung on the wooden
dowel suspended from a ceiling bar

Back and forth back and forth
and nothing no tune no song no peep

"Oy!" Yashke said, "no ordinary
jailbird, he..."

And:
"I too want to sing surely surely
or cry
Why don't I ha ha ha!!!"

Uncle Yashke coughed standing on
one leg like a stork gobs of
phlegm rode up and down
in his chest

Meemeh Chaye:
"Time to set the glass *bankes* on
your back..."

"why not castor oil?" Yashke asked
"That too," Meemeh Chaye said
Yashke shrugged and lowered
his right leg to the floor:

"*Ech Uchnem ech yuchnem...*"[9] he sang
and stamped off into his *varshtat*[10]

Listen to the song of the
Crystal chandelier the light
in the carved mahogany panels
the shadowed deep cornices under
the ceiling the shush of Meemeh
Chaye's pantoffles/my blond
cousin Layeleh playing a tralalalala in a half-dream
humouresque

Words gestures on
Purym nights...

A film being run
forward and backward
at one and the same time
to emphasize:

How do you do that?

With swivel *draydl*
the turning of
Purym top
self-inventing modalities...

With Mordechai and
Esther in the Throne-room
playing *patseh-patseh*[11]

Dying
so as to live somewhere else
                somewhere?

Two angels with portable wings
made of *Katshkeh* feathers (duck feathers)
squat in front of a
Francishkaner stork
discuss the ins-and-outs of sanctification
of going forth to see the

Dream-castles in hills
between one-way two-way mirrors of
reinvented
memories

*"Who provideth for the raven his prey
when the young ones cry unto God
and cry for lack of food"*

Blendung über blendung[12]
crossroads tied into knots
components of confusion

Do weavers still weave sunlit
stretches of silver haze
in Lodz?

A postal card picture of
Poznanski's Palace on Panska

lives in my dreams
surrounded by seven lions
           seven tigers
           seven rams
           seven bullocks

The red-brick wall
with glittering shards of blue
bottle-glass embedded into
gray concrete mortar
anthills
red ants...

inward outward
and up around

The high windows caught fire in the sun
beneath fringed kites

*"King Solomon made himself a palanquin
of the wood of Lebanon
he made the pillars thereof of gold
the seat of it purple ivory
the inside thereof being inlaid
with Love."*

My fair-haired cousin Layele
plays the piano in my head:
My mother's *Shtille Lieder*[13]

adjusting to the music-pauses
of silence upon
centuries of sorrow

Meemeh Chaye waits for me
every day on the second concrete
                              landing
with a brown paper bag
in hands
of the world's
wonderful chocolate
cookies

Once upon a time
          upon a time
Tateh vet koyfn shichelech
Meemeh vet bakn kichelech
Mameh vet zingen
Liederlech[14]

And Yashke danced with Layeleh
Chaveh and Soniah
round the long dining-room table

And now wandering about my
exile-street it is as if home
had never been

189

Zygmund

The Lord of the Pigeons on the
roof never told the truth
neither plus nor minus

He only had four flocks
of pigeons instead of as he said twelve –
        twelve minus eight

Zygmund climbed up the roof
to find a place
where nobody would see him cry

Not his father, mother
or sisters

The pigeons flew away
and Zygmund waited for them on the roof
day and night a
full week of days and nights —

                He rose to the top
                of the parapet and whistled
                and cried
                whistled
                and cried...

Unhappy with the taste of
salt tears in mouth

Below beautiful Veronika
Zygmund's sister drank on her

corner curtained-off cot
a full glass of iodine

Dreaming of burning rushes
in a swamp/hugging herself
in her own arms

Cast out of Eden Adam and Eve
squeezed ahead of the
                      Poznanski chimneys

The yarmulke cloud on the
top ladder rung
chimney fumes in throat
children on the
concrete pad

Zygmund waits for his
Pigeons on the roof

The cobbled road

the parallel gutters

Veronika on her cot

Good Tuesday day:
good for counting stone pavement cobbles
cracked concrete sidewalk squares
red apples in Matele's
koshykes

Pedestaled monuments
in City Parks

On the seventh day the pigeons
came back
reflecting fleetingly
in chintz-lined window-panes

Beating their homing wings

Zygmund rubbed his red-rimmed
eyes with gritty fists
and cried:

Good Tuesday Day
For rekindling dead coals
for victories in
shelter tunnels
for finding good sparks
in ashes
For cunning soccer-ball *kepkes*[17]
in wrong direction

In my good ear:
"*Do Palestyny!*
Do Palestyny"[18]

Good Day Tuesday on this side
                      on the other side
Along the green fence of the

coalyard facing Dluga Ulitsa
which runs parallel with
                      Konstantynovska
all the way toward Piotrkovska

My white goat with his
rusty short tail
and teak horns

slept under my crib

Mother sang:

Sleep *shluf ingeleh* sleep
under your little crib
sleeps a white kid

My white goat
advanced

I grabbed his teak horns
but he soon pinned me to the wall
and looked up:
take back your sins...
you damn son of Cain

My Nana Hyndeh sang:

Der tateh ys avek handlen
myt rozhynkes n'mandlen[19]

My mother sang:

Dus vet zayn dayn baruf
myt dem vet yideleh
handlen[20]

And:
An invisible synagogue
full of halleluya
hallelu
hallelu

At the feet of rubble
in dust...

193

Here's a drill
drill down to our house
in the
courtyard

Look down from windowsill
and up at the Temple Dome of the synagogue
on Kosciuszko street

The firebrigade stood by
clapping fire-hard
hands hurrah! hurrah! hurrah!!

The last letter from Nootl
dated with a shaky hand
February twelfth
nineteen forty-one
Balut Lodz
post stamped in Paris and
forwarded via paternoster post
to me from Toronto to
the airforce barracks
in Skudduc:

Moishe Moishe Vus Machstu

"Moishe Moishe vus machstu?
(how are you)
as if off an improbable
billboard
"In Balut yz bloyz TOYT
                bloyz TOYT!"
("Here there is only death")

"There were ten of us here
from our classroom in the Hebrew Gymnazium
in one stretcher
listening memorizing
remember?

'In the Basement
'in the Basement'

Against the window a dead wall
which ends the myth of light
from us altogether-forever

"I forget:
an unfinished thought!"

"We are now four

"Chatzkl Grabiarz and Betsalel Pogurek were
sent to Auschwitz
Shymshe the Lubliner died of
Tyfus Zudyck Kaminker was shot dead
while crawling beneath the barbed wire
fence to the other side...

the other SIDE
the other SIDE

"We found Menasheeh Cygleman   hanging
from a hook in the ceiling
in a neighbourhood
basement

"We saw him turning
in a single moonbeam
skin peeled off
as if he were a billboard

"We four are keeping daybooks
of forgotten thoughts
unconnected shooting disconnected
death in different
parts of the
GHETTO

"If one of us survives
he will have our daybooks
or know where they are

"Thoughts begin to turn in head
keep me awake

"Rats scratch in walls
bigger than cats

"A pyramid sits on my chest
go muscleman lift the pyramid
come Moishe Moishe
lift the pyramid."

God suffuses the sun:

flickering breath
fire tastes like horseraddish
in mouth of days
nights on the day
of my birth
day of birth: *Sheyshes Yemey Bereyshys*

It's as if in a dream
seeing you come to the window
and look at the bars
then look
at the wall in bluegrey light

You feel better?
Don't you?

Then God split the Red Sea in the
right moment of time
for the Pass-over

A little later
He drowned the Egyptian soldiers camels horses ele-
phants you can still see the steel helmets
in the constellation waves of
the millennia

1   *Kiechelech* – Cookies (Yiddish)

2   *Oodym haa'ryshon* – Adam the first (Hebrew)

3   Zyz – Gigantic mythological bird. The *Ziz* is so named because his flesh has many flavors tasting like this *(Zeh)* and like this *(Zeh)*. He is a clean bird fit for food and capable of teaching mankind the greatness of God. – Lev Rab 22.10 *Midrash Tehylym 363*

4   *Taddeusz Koscciuszko* (1746-1817) – Polish patriot; General in American Revolutionary army

5   *Polskie Woisko* – Polish army

6   *Adam Mickievicz* – Polish poet

7   *Visla* – Polish river

8   *Oz tus ... mayim* – And the vision dissolved like haze over water (Hebrew)

9   *Uchnem ech uchnem* – Hey hey pull together (from Russian stevedore song)

10   *Varshtat* – Workshop (Yiddish)

11   *Patsheh patsheh* – Clap hands (Yiddish)

12   *Blendung über blendung* – Blending over blending (German)

13   *Shtille Lieder* – Quiet songs (German)

14   *Tateh vet ... liederlech* – Father will buy little shoes aunt will bake cookies mother will sing little songs (Yiddish)

17   *Kepkes* – Head-shots in soccer (Yiddish)

18   *Do Palystyny* – Go to Palestine (Polish)

19   *Der Tateh ... Mandlen* – Father is always selling raisins and almonds (Yiddish)

20   *Dos ... Handlen* – This will be your fate (Yiddish)

22   *Dort zitct ... Alef-Bays* – There sits a teacher with little children he teaches the alphabet (Yiddish)

23   *Had Gadyu* – The little goat (Hebrew)

24   *Sheyshes Yemey Bereyshys* – Six days of Genesis (Hebrew)

SEVEN

"And Rip was slowly made aware
that he, Van Winkle, was not here
                    nor there."

I Look for Markers

I see my brother Layzer on the
inner windowsill counting fingers
on both his hands

Ayns dray zeks nahn[1]

search miseries
miseries search one another

in noose of weeping
in between maple floor
and belfry rafters

My father stares again again at his
stained forearms hands:
irregular blots of multi-coloured
skeins drip dye off woollens
silks and cottons

On second loft above
hardware store and butchershop

In the year of 1925

Tangled metaphors from
never before:
I begin to say no no no

Crisscrossed paths from Rudym to
Lublin to Lodz to Varshe to Gdynia
to Toronto Canada

The rivers: Bug Varta and Vistula
may never have existed
the countryside fields woods mountains
railway tracks may have existed
in the books of my dreams
in blue haze somewhere
Chugging locomotives
transporting
nights days
days nights – in cattle cars

old men doze: with hands clapped over ears
walk and fall
fall and rise
rise and die

again again
drifting
from Gdynia to Varshe
from Varshe to Lodz
from dream to nightmare
I break down and weep
again again

In Lodz I look for markers:
a school rucksack
my name on an exercise book
an empty pencilbox marked
Moishe Moishe

Engraved names on headstones
in cemetery

My city Lodz
its architecture

Piotrkowska Novomiejska Vschodnia Zachodnia
Dluga Panska Cegielniana Kosciuszko Zielona
City parks squares monuments

I touch with numb fingers numb heart
a frame of masonry
a panel a washstand
a rotted leg
of a Sabbath table
a brass sign
Moyshe Kohn engraved on a slab
of limestone

Around the Bend

Around the bend
No one waits

my zaide
my father
breathe anciently
faintly
drinking thirst of the universe
as thieves drink darkness
on steps of shadowed staircase

Chamitzhak Chamitzhak[2]
chants up the same staircase
about steel doors
barred windows

In pew
next to your pew
watching the wonder of the raising
of the Sabbath *Torah*
on platform

Two columns of fire
on this side
in light
filter through
stained windowpanes in haze
                    of archangel
                    wings

"*Asher kydishonu*"
"Because you have sanctified us"
                    sanctified us!
                    sanctified us!..

And Layzer
on windowsill
in front of bolted door
still counts

Ayns dray zeks fyier akht tsvay[5]

in my dream

The subsumed span
at gray edge of
dusk of edge of
moment that begins
with one who stands in
corner to witness in great din

In this dark sad city
mist rises out of cobbles
        Smokeless
        chimneys weave like masts
        above roofs away and gone

Yashke

In the end Yashke wrote letters in his head
walked all night
with my youngest brother
Layzer

Yashke:
"Listen carefully Layzer!
stay away from Balut

"Intentionally or unintentionally."

During the first night
they ran into a nightmare-forest
of a firing-squad

Layzer:
"Yashke will we die?"
Yashke:
"*Nnnnnneayn nayn.*"

Yashke:
"Entertainers dreamers mountain climbers
fortune-tellers little Jews
little gypsies:

"Run run run
through fiery hoops
through iron doors
iron bars

"Let me give you a hand up onto
your bareback horse
"Ride ride ride

into the blackest forest
in this sad dark world into the
wandering hours days"

Ravens

Excerpt from my Zaide's
teachings about ravens:

"Ravens were especially venerated and
shunned by our forefathers"

"In Job
God takes care of them
in Deuteronomy the (ravens)
are classed as unclean birds
in Proverbs they pluck out and
eat the eyes of the ungodly
in Kings they feed Elijah
in the Canticles
King Solomon's hair
is praised for being black
as a raven's wings."

In the wood Yashke Layzer and their companions
worked all kinds of magic during the long
nights

They might have built a fire
but that would involve all kinds of
risks Risks, risk-risks
at every turn in silence
                 of soul

And even though they felt besieged crushed
threatened and trapped out on a night-limb the gypsies insisted
on playing one of Hayden's sonatas
first in D natural then in D sharp then in D
between natural and sharp Layzer corrected

two or three notes in the D version "Too sloppy"
he said "even sentimental..." but the
first violinist a thin tall gypsy with
an oversized whispering fiddle said: "Listen"
that's the way he talked "Listen carefully to the
silence between the notes/it's what counts"
that's the way he talked "it
counts more than anything else/even in Hayden!"

Then with a profound expressful shrug as if to
say: What the devil *(do diabla)* do you want?

The listeners were humming buzzing and
vibrating fitting their thoughts together
            tearing them apart

But when the henchmen and the hunters
arrived it levelled
everyone to a heartbeat of one and three and five
skipping one beat in-between
instead of one-two/one-two/one-two/one-two
forgetting remembering

The chipmunks made themselves inconspicuous
betweenthetreetrunks and moss/the
rabbits went down into their holes the robins
lost their voices/the gulps in the gypsie's
throats ceased Yashke tried singing his belated
lovesongs Layzer wobbled his head counting:
"*Ayns dray zeks fynyf tsvay*"
the king gypsy whispered: "*tsvay fyier fynyf zeks*"

One of the Polish henchmen fully dressed in a light blue
uniform/highly visible even between trees kept
cracking his tigerandlion circus-whip
all the dogs were on leashes straining and barking

but the dog of the hunter with the
whip growled

The henchmen hunters and the dogs spread out in a wide
arc and surprised one another when they
arrived in the one spot from different
direction in a circular
clearing

Some of the gypsies hid inside mounds of dead leaves
others hid in hollows under halfburnt woodsheathing
and collapsed beams of a former hut
Distant voices sliced the
morning air with knifesharp commands:

"Achtung! Achtung! Judenraus rausraus"[7]

Through amplifiers

In the City

"One small satchel each no food and *raus*
shnell shnell"[8]

The streets were crowded with people
factory sirens shrilled

In the never bye of being – quick wings of dusk
in transcendence wings of morning light
feathers in wind
the circumstances evened straightened
knees turned into water/I can tell you
I can't tell you I wasn't
there My younger brother
Layzer Layzer was   there
Yashke was   there
I was   there
We were   there
    in silence
    in terror
    under open silk-blue
    skies —

If the curtains in windows
disappear blame someone
                    else blame...

Curtainless windows stare
at the opposite curtainless window
The tall gypsy snorts like a palamino

No one arrives in Balut to see
the sunset

without blinking
no blinking – why was the third
gypsy so tall???

The unboundedness unbinds
in broad daylight
into a downslope of sewage

Even the cats in the alleys stopped
yammering in their time of heat

everyone seemed too old
even the children in the beak
of the stork alongside the doubleflue
chimney on the roof
ran into
Tohu ve' bohu
Tohu ve' bohu[9]

Swallowed in
Sodom and
Gomorra

Ghosts
scrambled out of the pavement

They were not dangerous
they didn't complain
they didn't beg

They shuffled from Balut to Lodz from Lodz to Balut saying:
ummmmm ummm
rattling their bones.

They marked nightshadows nightframes nightsquares
darkblue nightwaves with fleshless fingertips

They followed the footprints of small children
they followed rats into basement ratholes

They marked doorposts
window shutters with King David stars

At dawn they drowned in a wild river
of remembrance

(This *breederl breederl* must be seen
It cannot be communicated by Morse
by Bell by Radar by prayers)

Tell the world that I am
signing off:

"'Goodnight *a gyteh nacht!*'"

Good Tuesday day:

Good for counting stone pavement cobbles
cracked concrete sidewalk squares
seconds minutes
Good for counting
red apples in Mateleh Shlyoch's
koszykes[10]

Now the white goat
sleeps under my cot
in the detention house
behind bars...

Now everyone kneeled to pray
but not everyone prayed
some stood and cursed
some couldn't stand
some couldn't pray

My father sat on a chair in a dark darkness
room

I said: Tateh
No answer
I said Tateh tateh!!!
He said: I am waiting for something to happen...

when nothing happened
he rose and switched on the light

I placed a memorized poem
under a bolted door
listened at the proverbial
keyhole to its
wall-to-wall heart

My father said:
If you keep this up
you will turn into a frog
If you play with the cat
your brain will turn into a catbrain
now and forever...

An old woman on the concrete steps
of the old stone church
looks down to the rosary in her lap
she then looks at me and says in a loud
axe-sharp voice: "Glory be to the father

and to the Son and to the Holy ghost
     and ever shall be
          shall shall..."

I saw distorted images of myself in the broken
bits of mirror in the sawdust/
silence repeats itself
I repeat myself
the children repeat themselves
We stare at the ghosts
          of dead
memories/I note that in between are
details/like the pump in the waterwell do you
remember Sroolekl at the windowsill closest to the
Midrash?

Reb Hersh on his way home from his
Bais Midrash stopped to tell me among other things
that everything is assembled according to
Gematria

again —
again —

God isolated Tohu with a bolt and
two iron doors (a double door with bars
shot across their wings)

This gives us a *terminus a quo* for the time
of creation
When I visited Yankeleh Sunshine
in the insane asylum in Toronto at nineninetynine
Queentstreetwest he told me:

Moishe *gay aroys n'zug di velt*[11]
that both Tohu and Vohu have
escaped from this place and they're
out there somewhere/and, godonlyknows where/or what they
    will do!

                                             what they

    will do!

I see myself in pallid
afternoon light at the window of a red
and beige streetcar heading home

Dreams live in dark darker alleys...

Circles squares triangles and trapezoids
merge and dance over cracked sidewalks

Mirroring thousands of faces
in good and evil light

some deaf
some blind
some dumb
some legless
some armless
some mindless —

Shadows fall back recede/together with
lanterns telegraph-poles balconied walls/
march with soldiers and storefronts

The streetcar sways from side to side
as the spool of the antennae connects
and disconnects as children group and
regroup on their way from school

play hide-and-seek bounce rubber-balls
skiprope/hairy dreams bloom above

The children's heads swing from
acacias to chestnut trees and always
the same neighing of Belgian horses pulling
draywagons with ballast

horses turn
into elephants with great ivory tusks
monkeys jump out of trees and dance dance

Chai on her way home with schoolbag
strapped to her back turns turning
indreamysilenceofhersilent song on toes
toetotoe arms apart to
embrace the poor dark dark unhappy world

At streetline at curb and gutter
a redfaced drunken Pole with his *bijak*[13] in
hand hops like a giant frog pounding
away at my friend Sroolekl ben Shloyme's
head shoulders face as they
turn in a wild dance

Sroolekl with face in
elbows trips at curb and lands face-down
in running gutter/as the Pole
smashes away at his head

I dreamt a paradise island with unexpected
mountains on the horizon

There were gardens with
roses tulips forgetmenots also
groves of fruit trees apples plums cherries
pears chestnuts/also bushes full of
ripe and ripening berries
and a tin can with a sprig of evergreen

There were little houses/shaded
by overhanging branches of trees but their
windows were shuttered and each house was
guarded by strange chained animals with human faces
They screeched "Gotohell gotohell gotohell!"

I threw a stone at one of them but my hand
together with my arm sailed away with the stone

When I came nearer I saw that a strange
chained animal was already gnawing at the bone of
my arm —

When I ventured a little further into the interior
round the rim of a purple mountain the land turned
into a wilderness/rocks weeds and craters
and only one man dressed in a long black robe
kneeled on a rock with
his hands locked in prayer

There were vultures and crows jackals and wolves
lions and tigers but they were all so thin they seemed
like shadows crawling in and out of weeds round
enormous craters of boiling black smoke

There were fish caught on giant hooks/blue gapers
silver sharks/shrunken whales/also little

catfish that hadn't even learnt to swim which
was a good thing because there was no water

I wanted to talk to the man in the black robe but when
I got to the exact spot where he prayed
He merged
with my solitude

I then climbed up a rock and
prayed to my skygod:

O skygodskygodskygod skygod
send me a wakeup sandman
          a wakeup sandman
          a wakeup sandman

But the skygod was not there
he was probably patrolling his seven
heavens round the other side
The faraway other   side...

I then set out to memorize a few
basically essential Biblical words:

Pres means 'earth' so does *adama*
and *arqu siyya* means 'dryness'/*yabasha*
means 'dry land'/*harabha* means 'parched
land'/*tebhel* and *heled* mean 'the world'
vilon means 'curtain'/*raqia* means 'firmament'
shehaqim means 'clouds' or 'grindstones'
zebhul means 'dwelling'

In My Dreams

In my dreams nothing is happy
there is no sandman
there are only squirming memories
And Chai's eyes searching my face

Above me the clouds
are even larger and grimmer than those
I noticed when I was born... when?

Reb Hersh runs on his long stiff
legs/the hinges at his knees
must have rusted
his gabardine cloak flies
behind him like a black crow's
wilding wings

The streetcar stops at the stop sign
and I run after Reb Hersh

Rope-ladders dangle
down iron railings
of storied iron balconies
Masked men with long spider legs
and small heads climb
up and down from balcony to balcony

In the midst of it all
in the courtyard
ceremonial dances
songs and stories arrange and
rearrange the afternoon's

scenery
of empty spaces

at a signal from one or the other balcony

Rain turns to snow
day turns to twilight
underpants get caught on
enormous hooks like fish out of rivers...

The sandman and ten of his
secretaries are facing
east in *myncheh maaryv*[14]
prayers

Tsy Farecthn

Layzer walks through
the bronze gates with a glazier's
box strapped to his back

Meemeh Chaye packs a satchel
with creams and lotions for
her trip to Balut

Layzer chants: *tsy farecthn tsy farecthn*
to mend to mend windowpanes window panes
       the world the world the world
       the roof of the world

Thousands of legs shuffle unshuffle from
Lodz to Balut

Layzer is dressed in old bleached trousers
with holes that show his swollen
kneecaps

The Poles line the sidewalks at the curbs
celebrating with ceremonial
dances songs stories
And Hurrahs hurrah!
          hurrah!!!

Layzer walks toward the head of the length of the line

Once there he raises a sheet of blue double diamond
glass and turns into a blue lantern

In my dream I met Layzer
in a yellow field
walking with poppies
through blue
mirrors

Layzerlayzer where are you going?
no answer

Tears run down his face
mix with mirror tears

O Layzerlayzer don't you know me?

Instead of answering Layzer
walks away with upraised arms

He chants:
Tsy farecthn tsy farecthn ayns dray zybn fyier
windows

mixture of tears
bring death into
the back of my eyes

In the blue mirror
In the blue mirror

A hundred women without wigs or hair
are being stoned by a mob of Poles

The bullseye turns into a ferocious tiger
with a red sun
in one eye

I am still waiting at the ruins of my Zaide's hut
for something to happen

The tiger arches his gleaming back looks at me
with squinting eyes
but nothing happens

"Adam and Eve
were driven out of the garden of
Eden on the first Friday of the week
in which they had both been created
and sinned

"On the first Saturday Adam rested
At the close of the Sabbath and prayed to God
for mercy

"He then went up to upper Gihon
which is the strongest river of all rivers

"There he served seven weeks of penance
standing in midstream with head upraised
with water up to his chin until his
body turned as soft as a sponge

"Afterward an angel came to comfort him
He taught him the use of fire-tongs
And a smith's hammer

He taught him how to manage oxen
so he shouldn't fall behind in his ploughing."

The angel meant well
but his thinking was
wrong all wrong wrong

1   *Ayns dray zeks nahn* – One three six nine (Yiddish)
2   *Chamitschak* – A portmanteau version of two Hebrew names: *Chayim* (life) and *Itzchak* (laughter)
5   *Ayns dray zeks fyier acht* – One three six four eight (Yiddish)
7   *Achtung* – Attention (German)
    Juden Raus – Jews out! (German)
8   *Shnell* – Quick (German)
9   *Tohu Bohu* – Empty and hollow (Hebrew)
10   *Koshykes* – Baskets (Polish)
11   *Gay aroys n'zug der velt* – Go on out and tell the world (Yiddish)
13   *Bijak* – Club (Polish)
14   *Mynche Maaryv* – Morning and night prayers (Hebrew)

EIGHT

"Heaven beg mercy for me!
if there is a God in you and
a pathway through you to this God
– which I have not discovered –
then pray for me!"
     – from *On the Slaughter*
       By Chayim Nahman Bialik

Adventure Time

In this blind City
columns of deracinated warriors
pour into the Parade Square

Hooked irrevocably face in hands
on knees before altar/stained glass/
flying red-and-white flags
maintaining distance
down the middle/the brass band

To the left the right about turn
one-two one-two
hands grasp at the moment of

The regimental tunes

O Maryszka moja Maryszka[1]

Alive enthralled
like the one I was with last night
with roar of battlefield in heart

One-ear-in-and-out-the-other
O Maryszka moja Maryszka

Forgot the time of
day week
and to whose
benefit to whose? to whose???
by whose command?

Layzer empties his pockets
turns them inside-out:

Veneer rolled on wooden spools/
a golden pocket-watch/
mercerized cotton skeins/
panes of leaded glass/
Yashke's engraved Sabbath cup...

He tells me about
what he forgot
what he remembers
what he left on shelves
in Yashke's *varshtat:*
in Goldsmith-
haze...

When he last made it up the
concrete steps of Yashke's flat

Janek Dziurny's wife Jadviga
opened the door:
no more than a crack...

She screamed:
"O Matka Boska
O Mother of God!
Mother of God!
go away   go back
         go back!"

And the walls stood about
breathing frozen memories
jawing on the meaning of
the word 'perplexed.'
        perplexed!..

A child inside
wailed children wailed
Like orphans in orphanage

And Jadviga:

"To nasze nie vasze
This house is   ours
      not   yours
Go back where you came from!"

In the Evening

In the evening my zaide
in his *Bays Midrash*[2] nodded over
a tome of *Pyrque Meshiah*[3] or a
tractate of the *Babylonian
Talmud*

(He told me once that
The story of the
Cities of Sodom and Gomorra which were divinely
destroyed in punishment for ungenerous
behaviour towards strangers is a commonplace
myth...
Perecydes records that Gortyna
in Crete was destroyed by Apollo for its
lawlessness
Ovid in his *Metamorphoses*
tells how an old Phrygian couple, Philemon and
Baucis hospitably entertained Zeus who spared
them from the catastrophe he visited on their
inhumane neighbours.)

When Layzer remembers the iron bars
in the windows of the Halifax Detention
house

He counts:
Ayns dray zeks tsvay fyier

When I tell him to stop
he turns into a cobblestone –
at
once

The Behemoth

My Zaide held that the
Behemoth resembles a prodigious hippopotamus
with a tail "bigger than the trunk of a
cedar" bones "like brass pipes..." "He
rules the earth's creatures the same as
the Leviathan rules those of the sea..."

Outside the City changes its harsh form and
takes on soft contours/grays become
slate-coloured and striped light green
yellow where the last light of the setting sun
still lingers/some windows in the courtyard
become bright with golden lamplight
My father is in the old synagogue saying his yearly
Kaddish for his father Moyshe Emes...

In the evening after the first star rose in
the sky I changed to a new undershirt/

I then said my night prayers rolling the words
in my throat from one breath to the
next —

Janek

Janek consults with cap in hand the Polish
heartbreak priest: I sinned

"O sinned father" shrill in ear
close to aperture/black beads
a golden icon boundround in blessblesses
clairvoyance:
"My son my son I am listening..."

Countless marginal sins: bad dreams/thoughts
of incest/threatened Jadwiga my own my Jadwiga
My wife with knife o father/
"And what else?"
"Robbed Jews during the war!"

"O my son that's not much of a sin my son!"

Things that already happened or still germinate
pendulum-like in poorpoor poorhead poowhirl...

Sins from green undergrowth risen from saplings
to trees wilding wheat that arrive and walk away
when the frosts set in

Consult the witch-doctor
in mirrored barbershop with his
scissors clippers and *tshymedantshyk*
filled with suction-*bankes* –

Think Way Back to Trip on Draywagon

To Czestochov
As many churchwindows
as stars in sky
mysticisms

On way

A nervous rabbit at entrance
of rabbithole
hooked on wiggly wiggledy
ears over its back and
no *arba kanfot*
no *arba kanfot*
no *arba kanfot*[4]

Listen to
approaching twilight flashlight
over path on steel-clad wood wheels crunching
over shussshing generations
of dead leaves twigs

A robber robbers behind an ancient oaktree with double-
    edged
knives – halt
the thunder of a behemoth with spiked
foot-thick hide falls back onto
himself as sky darkens with flight
of geese and weird prophecies open much larger
                        huger than promised Ziz
                        promised Ziz[5]

Legend Holds

Legend holds
that this gigantic behemoth roams
the thousand mountains
of the earth

Outroaring the fiercest
thunderclapping
from all directions

From the Poznanski wheatfields
textile factories
flatroofed tenements
park benches under summer and winter
nightstars scorched in firewood for
ovens
ovens
ovens

Pay Attention

The third blue fly
and the fifth blue fly
escaped the cobweb between
the door and the doorpost

The third and fifth
land on the
stone gargoyle's nose to
count stone dental courses

Pay attention:
Men and women climb up the
stone steps on bent knees
counting prayer beads
with dark burdened
hearts

On the way up to the loneliest of lonely
portals...

The dead sleep out of reach
      the dead turn to ghosts
      the dead turn
      the dead turn

Patshe patshe
clap clap hands wait for *tateh mameh*
on windowsill put all valid
questions
without limbs in old box...

236

Mother's unfinished Yiddish
novel sleeps somewhere in a cardboard
box

Yiddish heartbreak in every
chapter of commonplace workdays
wait for the Sabbath
the depth
of the waterwell in the rubbled courtyard

My brother Beyrysh measured it/it was/
bottomless

The spider went to the market
to listen to other spidery voices
different harmonies/goodmorning –
happiness dressed in patient happy
harmonies

Father
went to market
with bags of raisins
and almonds

Reciting:

Bumbledee bumbledee bumbledee
buzz buzz at the door of
the house

Reciting all the way
the tears of King David's
Psalms
Father went to market –

I should laugh ha ha ha should should:
but there he is the gigantic
Behemoth prodigious hippopotamus
with a tail "bigger than the trunk
of a cedar tree:" (look it up in your
Midrash: bones "like pipes of brass.")

It is disputed whether the Behemoth
was fashioned out of water or dust or light

Or was simply told by the Ruler of the Universe
to rise out of the earth

Rise out of the earth!

Some hold that the Behemoth
once had a mate
but he couldn't have coupled with her since the
offspring would surely have overwhelmed
the world...

God left the overwhelming to us
God left the overwhelming to us
                              us

                              us
                              US!

Others hold
that God prudently gelded the male Behemoth
and cooled the ardour of
the female but spared her until
the Last Days when her flesh will
delight the earth's righteous
        the earth's righteous
        the earth's righteous

The rows of the storied
windows in the walls suddenly brighten
with golden lamplight then die just as
suddenly one after another as if at –
a signal   at once

Who signals?
Where does the music come from?

One window
shone pure emerald

The music was not
really music it had no melody it was
a persistent humming ummmmmmmnhhhooooh
of primordial sadness

The gist of it was: whole but not fulsome
or wholesome
or wholesome
or wholesome

Squeezed itself up from the strange
strange throat-port/again again

Without the whale there would be
no Jonah was the whale created to
accomodate Jonah?

It seemed that whoever it was
had fortified himself with a large
bottle of Polish Vodka

Vodka is Poland's
favourite national drink

239

invented by
Batory
invented
      by a patriotic Pole
      or Jew
      or Jew
      or Jew

When night falls on my city Lodz the
acacia trees turn into a solid
dark green mass on oyster-coloured
trunks

The branches seem to embrace
one another and merge in darkness –
                    shallow shallower

Climb two
steps at a time to my uncle
Yashke and Meeme Chaye's flat
the door the door posts the *mezuzzah*
on the right door post

Uncle Yashke calls *"Kto tam?"*
I answer "Me Moisheh"

I say
Shulym alaychem shulym
they say *Alaychem shulym alaychem shulym Moishe*
                                   Moishe

I say Where are the children?
They say Are you really Moishe?

I say where is Layeleh Chaveleh Sonia Soorl Geetl Shaineh
Shaindl Goldeh Ryfkeh Nootl Loozer Loozer Nootl Haml
Matl Faigl Taibl Perl Hyndeh Zarbuvl Myer Yosl Yosl Fahvl
Chai

Chai Chai!
Layzer Layzer Layzer Beyrysh Mechl Shymsheh Lalkeh
Frandl Menasheh Roodl Hudl Shoshaneh Hadassah
Berl Shulamys Symcheh Matl Yankl Yoyneh Nuchym
Chuneh Boorech Brucheh Etl Layzer
Layzer   Layzer
Layzer!   Layzer
Fahvl Menachym Velvl Nechumeh Bashkeh Zysheh Zoodyk
Tsirl Chaneh Esther Layzer
                  Layzer
                  Layzer!
Shymyn Aarel Shuyl Kalmyn Genendl Baileh Ruchl
Shloymeh Gedalyeh Benjumyn Motl Itsheh Toyvieh Peysach
Avreyml Chai   Chai
        Chai   Chai
        Chai!   Chai

Have you heard from Beyrysh and Mechl?

I suddenly sneeze violently but unintentionally
they smile: *gezynt! gezynt!*

The brass samovar looms at the centre on
the kitchen table on a white embroidered
doily/whistles and puffs hot steam/in
front of me a plate of heaped high
chocolate cookies/I stare at the distorted
caricatured reflection of my face in the
brass samovar/Memmeh Chaye sits opposite

Me across the table to watch me (as my
mother once did) eat and drink/She turns
to Yashke with a golden smile that lights up her
face eyes:

Moishele always liked my cookies...

Yashke dances into the dining room as he
opens the door/I can hear the dzzzzin dzzzzin
of the old grandfather clock/Something's
terribly wrong/Yashke and Chaye seem much
younger than I am/somewhere their hearts
weep bone-bleach/Yashke dances round the table
with a bottle of Hungarian *Szlivovitz* in one
hand and three golden Sabbath cups in the other

Now that you are older Moishl
Let's make a *Le'chayim Le'chayim*
Le'chayim[6]
Let us make a
Le'chayim

Whose health?
Whose lives?

Silence settles on Meeme Chaye
She widens her happy hazel eyes/Yashke pours
wine into the samovar/past the old country
stores/the former bookstore the Shloymeh-
Shoolym's former butcher-shop the ruins of
the Scala theatre/the Poznanski Palace/glinting
shards of blue bottle glass set in concrete on top
of the brick wall past the wrought-iron ornamental
gates/synagogue walls move change perspective
turn hesitate want to leave
say good-bye/then walk down the circular

oak staircase/collapse into the dust of
rubble again again
        again again
        again again

There is something urgent somewhere
I feel it in my absent legbones
I want to go there past the
grayness/ messages telegraph in my
head/torture one another in arena of
battlement

Ghosts walk up and down steep-stepping
stairs leap over each other –
leap frog with faces in veils of gauze
made out of cigarsmoke/legs
like piano-wire zzzzzz zyzzyzzyz

They want to sleep in ashes in earth
like everybody else and why not why-
not in-sleptin-earth...

I want to go there past the gray
of barricades

spring summer autumn winter
and finally in good time lost
all my buttons in all my garments
one after another rotted timeworn threads
wrapped over rim of barethread

Found myself under
streetlantern corner in circle of yellow light
in nightshirt
highly visible

still stand there
with just one button
in my outstretched hand
slapping my face
with open palm: sinned-sinned-sinned

People pass
look the other way/one three five
eleven averted faces/a few press
copper *groshns* in my hand lift my
arm at elbow with one hand
and place coppercoin with the other
in open palm.

Ghosts stir in my veins saying
shushush with scalding energy/
point wounded toes at my head –

Invent absent plots

One button like a slice of
a fallen star a few *groshns* in
fist nothing against
the alleydark/things look
up at dome of cold stars/
frozen milkyway/lost scriptural
alefbays knots/and only one star/
brave spectacular arc
in sleepdream of inaudible
sound —

Nothing better than what for I write
nothing/according to primary know-
ledge of golden apple touching
the fringe of aura in my father's
eyes of pewsolitude in

sleepdream

Breathing truth
sold and bought at every corner of
the Novy rynek square
City merchants
on soapboxes high higher above tumultous

Crowd in unhappiness circle in circle of
yellow lantern light

Eyes in open saliva-crossed mouth/see
down to bottom of obverted fear in
darkbitter heart/only small fleeced sheep in mountain
at lower rim of sky dance round around
themselves into dark blithe splice-blue
spiked/on spire sword higher high/
than runaway shore of seven confounding
haven/heavens –

My uncle Yashke and Meemeh Chaye
are immaculately dressed/Yashke
in a stiff high starched collar
with a polkadot bowtie black tail
frock coat striped trousers and black
brush moustache/Meemeh Chaye in dark
purple dress flared at ankles/two
silver foxes over bare shoulders a diamond
tiara in golden tight knot-laced golden
hair

Beyrysh laughs throaty trilling
laugh: "A couple of bourgeois ha ha ha
burgjashs/A shajnem dank – Thank you – Dank
                              Thank you – Dank

Yashke and Chaye hold hands as they climb up windowsill
climb up leaning shoulder to shoulder
in cleareyed survival
How could it ever be otherwise/no one could
imagine this otherwise/only one way to
clear wide window through opened
wings of casement
in this abstractious life

Yashke laughs *Zaytmer gezynt*/be happy healthy
and well he grows instantaneous
                    wide wings wings
Black-bat wings between shoulder bones through holes in
black frockcoat/Meemeh Chaye cocks her tiaraed
head to side and sings tralalalala alllaaaella/
wait for me wait for me – together
in cool blue haze of evening autumn air
under stars lallsllalllalhhh

I still see Yashke with golden *kiddush* cup in
hand raised high above his head singing:
        L'Chayim l'chayim
        l'chayim l'chayim
        Die Gantzeh Velt – The whole
                        world all living
                        Day in this antiquated life

Whose health whose health whose health whose wealth whose
    life in
this blind mute world world world

Whose life do I live?
            I live?
        do I live?

246

Apertures of Escape:

Try to locate yourself
among protective walls
under a billion stars

Through passages from
past appellations

Facing East into Hallucination

Messages on walls
writ with bleeding fingers
Letters to the outer
world packed into cardboard boxes
at knees – like beads of oozing vista

Tepid muted thumpthump
inside walls of garden
of many colours

Someone wants to get out
Someone's had enough
thump-thump of
Drone-drum

Another asks: Are you still alive
thumpthumpthump Are you
Alive? all day day/day all

At any price in any dream –
Chai turns into a halo
over a rosebush of sorrowfull
elegance

When the petals withered Chai
went to sit in her heart's clinkers

Out the window she could see
snowballs and snowmen in circular
war-room

In my memory
the *Midrash* Behemoth leaves a furrow-
like wake/which spreads far and wide
further than the distance between
Tiberias and Susita on the opposite shore
of lake Gennisaret/
through all cloud-pillars

And oh well hell here you are
figure this out for yourself
on the Middle East map hand-
drawn in Indian ink
in silver threads of moonlight
out of living in full-stride-swerve

I listen with my seethrough disproportion-
ate ears/pink in any old light/eyes
peeled at exile landscape of a thousand
islands/listen to fractured remnants
of doe-eyed song widening as the trapdoor/opens closes
ever so slowly at my bare frostbitten
feet/in this space measured by
span of right frozen hand
        right hand bones
        right hand out of the living bones

In this blindmute space

See a backtilted face with black knitted
eyebrows and cigarette in corner of lipstick
smeared mouth inventing new plot newer plots

And one of those strange noses readying
forever-and-ever to Tryioooo Tekyiooo
by precise notes engraved in flare
of folded nostrils/downward and up drawn
in spiral of agony – of celestial
chimney smoke float

I bow I click my bare heels
O where are my calf-leather shoes
why am I shoeless/click blue spurs instead of
knee-click/I form my mouth in sequence of
metronome click/in spite of everything I show
a savage crooked smile/I should put on my
solitude mask to show I'm not afraid

Sundays Mondays Tuesdays

These rows of saintly stone faces
mascaraed with soot along the roof parapets
gossip cynically before light dies/as raised
eyebrows pass from one to another/others others

Most especially on Sundays/Sundays are better
than Mondays/Tuesdays are better than Sundays and
Mondays/I examine the faces of weekdays
and Sabbat Days

Chai from Latvia Veronika from Cienstochov
Shulamit from Montreal Haddasah from New York
Zisl from Philadelphia Kay from Vancouver – whoever
remembers the rest –

The gray donkey from the Carpathian mountains
may be too tired on any of the above-mentioned
days/too much
mountain climbing a full childhood of
mountainclimbing/blue flies ants countless
insects nameless nocturnal earthworms – climb

I once knew how to cut an earthworm in two for
fishing bait: kneel in sand on shore of
brook with fishhook in one hand and a
halved wiggly earthworm in the other...

When I returned home my father waited for me
at the front entrance He said: Where were you?
I said: fishing/caught
a dozen fish
he said: take them back this very

minute. I said: why why???
he said: We buy fish in a fishstore!

Sundays are better than Mondays!

When I finally got home the cat Masha was playing with
a spool of thread/when I looked at her a knitting
needle punctured her left nostril...

Tuesdays are better than Sundays Mondays
                              and Wednesdays

Owls are lonely on limbs of trees they
call out to reassure themselves in misunderstanding...

Old men with tobacco-stained beards
sit together on a bench under the milkman's
window/their shadows stretch ahead/
Women arrive with empty pails to
fill them at the water pump

Where is the waterpump – singsong
where is the street – singsong
where is the house – singsong
where is Chai – singsong

The old men on the bench
suck their gums and count the buckets of
water dripdrop

The owls in the coalsheds
the sparrows among the stone cobbles/the stone cobbles/

the sparrows on the laundry lines in the
courtyard/

One old man prophecizes: "He heh/you
mark my words The Meshyiach will be
here among us/'n less than a year..."
Another is more hopeful: "No no no a year is too
long how about six months... ech???"
A third says: "Next week make it next
week... please God..." Breathing
                        Together

The third says: "I will settle for next week" then
rubbing his dry hands together: "*Oy kinder* (children)
kinder kinder let's stop countin'
Don' you know or did
you forget next week six months a year ten
years is in god's hands... So?"

All day day long

Staszek the drayman sits high up on his
draywagon/old before his time/older
than his horse *kalikula do diablo Kalikula*
FATHER
MOTHER OF DEVIL DEVILLED
                        BEDEVILLED

He cracks his whip and curses

Scratching with the other hand the fatty deposits
on his belly also the left ribs
foreknown by virtue of itching but
nothing/not anything/nothing...
all day day long

The horse lowers its head down to its front
wobbly knees/shrinks inward in spasms
through pulsating underside/collapses...
on his side/skeletal belly throbs in layers
and layers of moisture at the curb
and finis...
enough's enough in the middle of the salient month of
May of cardiac arrest...

I smell mother's beetborscht on stove
whiff of vinegar catches in my throat/the horse's eyes
are already full of flies/bats a bit off
circle in coalshed/my white goat climbs down
the roofshed to tell me he is homesick/
unfurled red and white flags
move past
gray walls/a crow with upraised
wings takes off/there's
a jasper field on the other side of the railway tracks
with worms fireflies in daisy hearts

My Zaide's wood was already burning when the firemen
rang their bell-clappers/a Polish policeman sights
down the barrel of his gun at the crosshair
on my forehead/Roosters with bloodred combs kukur-
    rrykoooh

I pray and the mournful grandfather-clock with its
brass heart prays with me dzzzzzz dzzzyndzzzyn stacato insis-
    tence
dzzzzzz as the minute-hand circles the round
face with the roman numbers round and around
the root of death —
Pray pray – pray for me

At midnight the dervishes and the ghosts gather round the
        water-well in sustained despair
in the courtyard

I am on my way to
Yerusholayim via Leningrad Moscow Vladivostok Toronto
        Halifax – Lodz
. through and above the billowed cloud
formations/to look for my brothers:
Beyrysh Mechl and Layzer

God caught the Leviathan with a hook/
hurled him up from the deep/tied
down his tongue with a rope/thrust a reed
through his nostrils/pierced his jaw with
a thong as if the mighty Leviathan were
a mere river-fish

Somewhere in the shadows under the
beams and the rafters someone rocks a
cradle:

          Rockabye baby baby by
          lullabye lulla
          lulla lulla baby lull
          lullable in able
          cradle of
          garden flowers/
          garden flowers

In swath of sweeping sun a billion (maybe)
miles up I enter the ruin through a gate on
rusted hinges on post of graffiti fence full of

snakes with gargoyle heads:
Hum of the dead

A blind man walks into my memory
with hand
stretched in front of him

A hundred blind men
walk forward with
hands stretched
in front of them

My own knees
No longer bend around
the bend

Only a few steps forward
a few steps backwards reciting a memorized *Kaddish:*
Isgadal ve'iskadash magnified sanctified:
Holy holy holy in every dark place places

Then forward towards the charred
lives/thinking about
how to say goodbye along throttled
dotted line of new paranoia/
splinters of cradle our old clock
in corner/the oak dining table with six
leaf extensions/the shards of the glass-front
bookcase bits of leather bindings/indecipherable
scraps of *shaymys* still inflammable kindling
used to start the fires in stoves in hearths of
ovens

in mother's *prypetshyk brent a
fayerl* was when I took my shoes and socks off

to bathe my feet in *balyeh* of rainwater/
Firewood used up during second world
war that still churns at every reinforced
corner/

In time time time in liaison
time spread at feet/bowed in shame of
unspeakable lies/barefoot and no
rainwater during the full months of June July drought
and lies at all points

When I awoke out of my nightmarish sleep the
mirroring words drowned and I felt the Behemoth's
whiskers on my cheeks
The creature smiled at me
and at the self-portrait in his hands/ah that
that and something else on his mind in both
hands by extension but never never mind

Rover rides away in four horse
carriage full of chlorophyll/toothless maidens eat
out of a common "blueplate"/a
dry seaherring from Lithuania in centre of
                                        the centre
                                        of centre

And I
worry about how to say finis
final goodbye words

with a little
        cheroseths
        horseradish
        tobasco

shankbone
egg dipped in saltwater

Ready to crossover to the other disproportionate side
of the miracle-sea with round *matzoth* baked in
Reb Yosl Hurvitz's bakery in Lodz/and sphere
discs of golden dots
turned black —
before eyes

On Window Sill

My head shrinks to
size of MacIntosh apple walnut

Plum blueberry

Beneath milky way
and bittersweet stars

     Eyes in all three corners
     in fourth a weeping
     Meshyiach with face in palms of hands

     On
     mourning footstool...

No time for new game
too many inclement messages
might be the last draw/white sheets cover all mirrors
voices rise and fall in shimmer – sackcloth and ashes

And rainbow arc choreographed
by God's *Meshyiach* Ben Joseph/Ben David in mourning

In fields wheat rots
Along the railway tracks/on the other
side of my Zaide's wood/satyrs
sing hold hands and dance dance

In the evening
God's curtain falls
in shimmer of eventide

Then one satyr runs
another takes off in a copter whirl
a third falls
again again

And that's me
on the windowsill
with knees up to my chin

And two asterisks above the
knees sing:

Let me go go go... this day day this...

Arms clasp throbbing thighs
legs   my bones grow
                grow
                grow

mustn't let them escape
must let them escape
                escape

Out of their longago
from goal
to goal

Hynde and the children are sound asleep
        each dreams own dream on
        own bed under mushroom
dome of Mother's parasol

Damp childish regenerative dreams

259

Catch a good luck iron ring in neverland
reach all the way out with
one hand clutch the turning
carousel-post

Turning head turning
ringaround around
around
the garden colours
of the world of belching chimneys

Shtainerne Palatzn Ayzerne
balko-konen
Stone castles
iron balconies
copper turrets

hanging in reaches of
good evil
secret

Beyrysh and Mechl are out
measuring the crossroads
building phantom
barricades

We are in The Halifax
Canadian Detention House
Waiting for Chamitzchyk – Chaim-Itzchyk

1 *Maryszka moja* – My Mary (Polish)
2 *Bays Midrash* – Study house (Hebrew)
3 *Pyrkey Midrash* – Midrash on the Messianic glories of the
    Yerusholayim Temple in Israel
4 *Arba Kanfot* – 4 Fringes (Hebrew)
5 *Ziz* – Mythological bird (Hebrew)
6 *L'Chayim* – Toast to health (Hebrew)